Love's Amazing Grace

The Reunion

C.A. Simonson

A Simonson

2015

Book III of the Journey Home Series

Aspen Run Press

Copyright © 2015 C. A. Simonson

CreateSpace.com

ISBN-13:978-1517460723

ISBN-10:1517460727

Cover Design: C.A. Simonson
Photo credits: Jo Beechner and Photobucket

DEDICATION

This book is dedicated to family and the power of relationship, love, and prayer. Someone once said, "a family that prays together stays together." The bond of agreement between two or three along with unwavering faith promises to always bring wondrous results.

ACKNOWLEDGEMENTS

I am grateful to my husband who encouraged me to write this third book. I am also grateful for the many friends who spurred me on by asking when it would be finished. Thank you to Penny Kubitchek, who helped edit, and to others who have given wisdom in the publication of this book. As the author, I hope you have enjoyed the *Journey Home* trilogy – it was my journey as well.

Table of Contents

C. A. Simonson

CHAPTER 1 - A FRANK TALK

Dol grumbled to herself as she heard the telephone ring. *Should have thought to put a phone in the sewing room too.* She stopped the sewing machine to head for the kitchen. She picked up the phone, and poured herself a cup of coffee. "Hello?"

"Hello, Dol!" Frank's voice held an edge. "Know you're busy. Have bad news."

"What's wrong? Everything okay? It's been months since I've heard from you."

"Sorry I haven't kept in better touch. Been tracking down clues about Guy's whereabouts since I was there last year."

"Almost a year and a half, brother," she corrected. "Timmie is eighteen months old now. I still marvel how God sent you to me when I needed you. I could have died in childbirth if you had not been here to deliver the baby."

"I'm glad we found each other too. But this is serious news – bad news. I think I might have found Guy. Maybe you'd better sit down."

She caught her breath and pulled a chair close to lean on. "Go on."

"Remember the letter I got from Guy? It was postmarked California. He said he had joined the Navy; had to write a final letter home."

"I remember. He sent it to the Johnsons'. They had saved it for almost two years because they didn't know how to find you. They were happy when you came back to visit Tekamah. I think of how horrified we were to learn why he wanted to get away."

"Me too. I checked the recruiter's office in Omaha, the closest one to Tekamah. They said all Navy men went first to Chicago for basic training and from there to Virginia."

"That still doesn't explain California."

"Many ships sailed from California: the *Midway,* the *California,* the *Yorktown,* to name a few. I've searched through the rosters of all the ships. The U.S.S. *Yorktown* was the only one to sail from the dock in Virginia around through Panama to San Diego, and then out to the Battle of Midway in the South Pacific. There was one man on *Yorktown's* roster named Ervin G. Larue."

"Frank, you're quite the private eye. I'm proud of you! But this all sounds like good news." Dol took a sip of coffee. "Why do you think it's Guy?"

"He was the only Larue onboard from Tekamah, Nebraska."

"Then it has to be him. But why would he have changed his name to Ervin?"

"Maybe he didn't want anyone to find him."

"Because of what he said in the letter...?" "That was my first thought."

"Did you find out where the sailors from that

ship went after the war?"

"Well, brace yourself. Here's the bad news. The *Yorktown* was bombed by the Japanese only weeks before the end of the war. It sank."

Dol gasped and collapsed into the chair. Hot coffee burned as it spilled onto her lap. "Sank?" Her voice caught in her throat. "Any survivors?"

"It appears there were some, but not...." He choked as he swallowed the last word.

Dol was silent as she gasped for air. *This can't be. God, please. Not another brother gone...if there's any way....*"Are you for certain...Guy was onboard?"

"I hope and pray he was not, Sis."

A few seconds ticked away as Dol choked away the sobs.

"Dol, are you okay?"

"I don't know if I can handle this...." Her voice cracked. We were abandoned and left to fend for ourselves. Frank hopped a train to get away from abuse; I was forced to leave the orphanage after Josie and Grace were adopted. Mike and Jesse were safe with the Johnsons only to have them die young. Guy went to look for Pa, but instead joined the Navy because he thought he had murdered him. "It's...it's just too much...." Her voice faded.

Frank took in a huge breath. "I know. We'll get through this, Sis. I want to trust God has spared our big brother. If he's alive, we have to find him and let him know he's innocent – that Pa didn't die at his hand. I promise to keep searching."

"And I..." Dol pulled herself together with a huge breath, "...will continue to look for Josie and Grace. I've begged the orphanage to give me information on them, but they won't budge.

"Don't you have some sort of privilege since you make and mend the children's uniforms?"

"Apparently not."

"Didn't you tell me you were there only a few months?"

"Yes. We three girls were processed into the orphanage in late October, 1936. The orphanage separated us and made the younger girls live on a different floor. I barely saw them. Two months later, the girls were adopted. My heart broke." Dol's voice betrayed her sadness as the memory flooded back to the day she watched the girls leave. Grace had been excited, but Josie had to be forced into the car. Dol envisioned Josie's little face pressed against the back window, screaming. Almost fourteen years ago now. So much has happened. Grace would be eighteen now, Josie, twenty. *Wonder where they are now?*

Dol wiped away a tear at the memory. "After all these years, there are many new personnel. They see me as an outsider trying to get information – one thing they do not give out freely."

"Is that administrator still there you told me about?"

"Marva Smarkel? Yes, she's still there. Must be

in her sixties by now, and still single." Her heart beat against her chest with renewed anger as she remember how the skinny old spinster kept her sisters' adoption from her. Dol's mind's eye saw the old maid with her hair piled on top of her head like a bird's nest, and wire-rimmed glasses perched on her bony beak of a nose. She smiled in spite of herself. She never did like the old warden.

"Well, long-distance costs are climbing, so I must say goodbye. Keep the faith, Sis. With God's help, we'll find the rest of our family."

"I won't give up hope, dear brother. I still marvel at how He brought us back together after all these years. If God wants our family back together again, He'll help us find the way."

"It was quite a miracle, wasn't it? I thought I was meeting a seamstress to hem my trousers. Little did I know it would be you. God works in mysterious ways."

Dol nodded, overcome by emotion. "Keep in touch, and let me know if you find out any more news on Guy. Oh! One more thing. The orphanage did tell me something peculiar about Josie."

"What?"

"They have no record of a Josephine Larue. She was adopted with Grace. Why wouldn't there be any record of her?"

C. A. Simonson

CHAPTER 2 - NIGHTMARES

Huddled in a secluded corner of the ship, Guy hugged his knees, shaking with fear and cold. The total darkness threatened to consume him. His eyes hurt from crying, his body ached from fighting. He jerked as another rat tried to seek refuge beneath his jacket. He was alone. Abandoned again. Left to die on a sinking ship.

He wrestled with the bedsheets that felt as if they would strangle him. Drenched in sweat, his body twitched as the vivid nightmare tormented his soul.

Planes flew in every direction. Flames, tracer bullets, and explosive bombs blew the enemy apart. The sky, black from anti-aircraft fire, stung the eyes and burned the nostrils. Plane fragments collided in the air. Firing continued. As shells careened past each other, it was difficult to distinguish incoming bullets from those being fired. Fear engulfed Guy Larue, an airplane mechanic on deck, but bravery and stamina overrode his fright. The sailors fought on, not knowing it would be their last battle at sea.

The U.S.S. *Yorktown* shuddered as the first bomb detonated on deck. The force of the blast flung Guy's body through the air and bashed him against the water main so hard it smashed. Dazed and confused, he was unaware of his surroundings; his legs were tangled beneath his body, his clothes torn open. Three planes on the flight deck exploded and fires broke out everywhere.

"Donner, get your plane in the air and blast those bloody Japs," Guy heard somewhere in the distance. Vaguely aware, he saw his friend Jack run toward his B26 bomber and take off.

"Larue, get up and douse those flames!" Captain Buck yelled.

Guy pulled himself up and joined the battle to put out the fires. He heard the roar of a plane. As he looked up, his eyes widened in fright as a Japanese bomber dove straight for the aircraft carrier. Jack shot the plane down and as it disintegrated, its bomb fell toward other bomber jets on deck. Guy froze in horror. *If that bomb hits the Dauntless, we're goners.* He panicked. It was fully fueled and armed with a one-thousand-pound bomb.

"We'll make it, Guy." Tink's voice rose above the din, as if in a dream. "Have faith, man."

"Tink—you're hit. You're hit!" Tink sunk to the floor as shrapnel flew through the ship's gaping wound. A blank look crossed Tink's face as he tried to make sense of the searing pain in his chest.

Guy jerked awake. Sweat saturated his trembling body and fear threatened to take his soul once more. He tried to shake the dream, but its reality continued to haunt him night after night.

Guy showered, pulled on his clothes, and hiked the quarter mile from his barracks to the Engine Mechanics Technical School at Lincoln Army Air Force Base. He immersed himself into his work of training other airplane mechanics in hopes it would shake his nightmares. It didn't.

His lips tightened into a thin line with the memory of the last encounter with his father before he ran away to enlist – the argument, the fight, the fatal blow. His forehead crinkled into a frown. *Why did I have to hit Pa so hard?*

Lost in thought, he didn't hear his co-worker come up behind him. *And why did Tink have to die? It should have been me, not Tink. I should have sunk with the ship.*

"You okay, sport?" Jack slapped him on the shoulder. "You were somewhere far away just now. You've been in the dumps for weeks now."

Guy forced a smile. "It's nothing. Been having nightmares – bad war memories." The smile faded as he turned back to his work.

"We Yorkies have to stick together, Bud. We've been through too much together."

Guy agreed. "Sure glad you decided to come back to Nebraska with me."

"Ah, well, we could hide out in Hawaii only so long, right? When they shipped us back to California, I thought my girl was waiting for me, but no such luck. When you asked me to come to Nebraska with you, I wasn't sure. You already had a job waiting for you as an airplane mechanic, but I was a pilot. Then when I found out the Technical Training Command School was here and there was a job open as a trainer of new pilots, I knew I had made the right decision. I can only thank you, my friend."

"You were a mighty good pilot, Jack, but they still got us. Sunk the ship. We lost a lot of good men."

"Shooting down Japs was the highlight of the War, but I feel bad about the men and the *Yorktown* too."

"Never did know his name," Guy changed the subject.

"Who?"

"Tink, one of the other airplane mechanics on board. He was a close friend and co-worker. Tinkered with stuff all the time, so we called him Tink; the name stuck and that's all I ever knew him by. Can't stop thinking of him."

"Lucky someone found you two, or you both would have sunk with the ship."

"We didn't know everyone left."

"You didn't hear Captain Buck order everyone off the *Yorktown*? He thought everyone had gotten off. Didn't see you on board, so figured you'd already gone into the drink. But no." Jack closed his eyes and shook his head. "You had to stay behind."

Guy shrugged his shoulders. "Someone had to stay with Tink. We tried our best to mend the ship, get her going again, but then the third bomb hit. Tink was severely wounded. When I realized we were alone on a sinking ship, I thought for sure we'd die out there on the ocean...." Guy's voice trailed.

"Alright, you two. Back to work," their boss surprised them from behind. "This ain't party time."

"Sorry, boss." Guy apologized. "Just reminiscing."

"All you sailors are alike – chewing your chaw about the war. Save it for after work."

"Yes sir," they echoed in unison.

"Let's meet up after work for drinks at Duffy's. How about it?" Jack slapped his pal on the shoulder. "Heard they have girls down there."

"Sure, I guess. Guess I could use a distraction."

Jack grinned. "Settled, then. It'll do you good. You'll see." He put his arm around Guy's shoulder. "We'll ride together."

C. A. Simonson

CHAPTER 3 - STUCK AT DUFFY'S

Jo brushed the stray curls from her face, tired of it all. She wished her life could go away. From the first time John McMillan had picked her up and forced her into his car until now, the only way she could survive was to comply with his wishes. She refused to call him Dad, Pa, or anything else that remotely sounded like "Father." He was no father to her. Life was hard and she hated it.

Jo bore down on the stubborn stain on the bar counter. Duffy's Bar & Grille was the last place she had ever dreamt of being. She hoped to become a nurse someday, not wipe down tables. Her knuckles were red and raw. *My hands wouldn't look like this if I'd stayed with the McMillans.*

"Jo. Order up."

Jo stopped rubbing the stain and rolled her eyes. "Right away, George."

Out of the corner of her eye, she had seen six men come in and sit down. *Another group of rude servicemen, no doubt.* She hated this job. Jo promised herself she would quit when she had enough money to move somewhere on her own. For now, she would have to put up with rude men and the off-colored comments they threw her way.

She served the burger and fries to the young

couple at table four. The blonde woman's hair was pulled back into a stylish ponytail. When she turned to look up, Jo did a double take. The lady's sky-blue eyes and facial features brought back visions of her older sister, Dolly. She gawked at the woman.

The woman looked bewildered. "Miss?" she shifted uncomfortably in her seat as Jo stared. "Are you all right? You look as if you'd seen a ghost."

Jo jumped and struggled to regain her composure. "Oh, my. I'm so sorry...I'm fine. It's just that...well, you look like my sister. You caught me by surprise, that's all," Jo blushed in embarrassment. "Please, forgive me for being so rude."

Jo shook herself mentally as she walked away, but the vision of Dolly remained etched in her mind. How she missed her! Her sister had always been there for her. She had watched out for Grace and her, cared for them, nurtured and taught them.

Thoughts of family tumbled through Jo's brain. She also missed her twin brother, Jesse. He had always been sickly, and she worried whether the Johnsons were taking good care of him. The last she knew, that is where Guy took Mike and Jesse when the seven siblings split apart.

She wondered whether Grace had forgiven her for the angry words spoken between them the last time they were together. She hadn't had a chance to make amends before she left. She worried about

Grace, especially with John, their adoptive father. Grace was too trusting – and too gullible for her own good. John McMillan had looked so handsome and kind when they first met him – so unlike their pa. *If I had only known what I know now...*

Jo poured six glasses of water, put them on her tray and clenched her teeth. *Be professional and polite,* she told herself as she forced a smile for the servicemen at table six.

C. A. Simonson

CHAPTER 4 - THE DRESS

Grace turned a 360, inspecting her petite five-foot-one image in the full-length mirror. She tugged at the low bodice and frowned.

"Too low, don't you think? Maybe a pinch too tight too," she noted as she turned sideways.

Joan admired the reflection of her younger daughter. "How beautiful you've become, Grace! You'll make a gorgeous bride."

Grace was radiant as she tried on one wedding dress after another. She glowed with excitement at her upcoming nuptials. She had flourished and grown in the McMillan home over the past fourteen years. William, her fiancé, was the perfect young man: handsome, affluent, brilliant. He more than met the McMillans' approval.

The attendant brought another gown. "How about this one?" she asked.

Grace's nose wrinkled at the cream-colored chiffon gown with puffy sleeves and hoop skirt. She rolled her eyes at her mother with a slight shake of her head.

"Oh, go ahead and try it on," her mother prodded.

Grace made a face as she complied and slipped

the hoop skirt over her head.

Joan McMillan's mind drifted back to the day they adopted Josie and Grace.

They had wanted children for so long – or at least she had. They tried to conceive for years, but it was not meant to be. Joan had become despondent and depressed as her biological clock ticked away. Miserable to live with, she was hopeful when John suggested a visit to Overbrook Orphanage to look for a little girl. She finally began to pull out of her doldrums.

When she spotted four-year-old Gracie Larue, she knew she had found her perfect prize. Grace was a gem from day one with her golden curls, fair skin, and blue eyes. She was cute, sweet, and compliant. Then there was Josie.

Joan's reverie was broken when Grace returned to model the poufy dress for her approval.

"Mother, this just isn't me." Grace turned up her nose.

The attendant brought another armload. "I'm running out of wedding dresses, Miss," she teased. "Maybe one of these will do."

Grace took the dresses and headed back to the dressing room. A few minutes later, she glided from the dressing room with the train of her gown flowing behind her.

"What do you think of this one?" Grace turned slowly. She stroked the white lace-over-satin, pearl-trimmed gown. Her face shone with pleasure.

"Grace Ellen, you are stunning!" Joan put her hand to her mouth. "We'll have the seamstress create a veil and headpiece to match. Add some elegant pearls and you will be all set."

Grace turned the price tag over in her hand and gasped. "Are you sure we can afford this?"

"Anything for you, dear Grace. Anything. You are mine to spoil."

Grace sighed as she gazed at the heap of wedding dresses in a pile on the floor. "I can't decide. Mother, I really don't like any of these, and this one is way too expensive. I'd rather have something simple, sleek, something that flows gracefully."

Her mother smiled. "Just like you," she commented. "You will glow in any dress, honey."

"Maybe we can go to Martin's Wedding Shoppe? You know that fancy store in Omaha? They'd have a bigger selection."

"Of course, darling. We'll plan a trip soon. Anything you want. Money is no object."

Grace's mood dulled. "Thanks, Mother, but what I really want is for Josie to come home for the wedding. I want her to be my maid of honor."

"I know. I know, dear. But it's way too far away for her to come all the way home."

"Could we at least call and ask her?"

"We'll have to ask your father, dear." Joan squirmed in her chair. She knew Josie wasn't too far away, although she didn't know exactly where.

As Grace went back to slip out of the wedding dress and back into her street clothes, Joan remembered the day the adoption was finalized. Although they hadn't planned on adopting two daughters, the orphanage wanted to keep the girls together. She was more than thrilled; two girls would complete their family. She would have a daughter to spoil, and so would John. *I hate to think we actually shopped for daughters, but that's what we did. Money was no object then, either.* Joan bemoaned the thought.

Josie hadn't wanted to be adopted, and fought to stay at the orphanage. The girl never seemed to like our home and had run away several times. *Why? Both girls were treated equally. Well, that's not altogether true. I've spoiled Grace a whole lot more than John did Jo.*

She remembered how both girls mourned for weeks when they were first adopted. She told herself it was just a phase. One day she learned there was an older sister left behind, and before going to the orphanage, Josie had lost her twin brother. No wonder Jo is so defensive. *Wonder where Jo is now?*

"Ready, Mother?" Grace's voice jerked Joan back to the present.

"Oh, my. I must have been daydreaming. Yes,

I'm ready."

"Would you speak to Father, then? About Jo coming home, I mean?"

Joan sighed. "Yes, of course, darling. Whatever you want."

C. A. Simonson

CHAPTER 5 - HAUNTING MEMORIES

"Invited a few guys. Hope you don't mind. They want to hear some war stories from real sailors who've been there," Jack made his eyes big.

"Sure," Guy cocked his head and shrugged. "The more the merrier."

"Don't worry, bud. I told them to call you Erv."

"Suppose it doesn't matter anymore. When I joined the Navy, I went by Ervin. Wanted to be a different person, you know?"

"Well, no, I don't know, but we'll keep you a secret for now."

Duffy's Bar & Grille sat on the west edge of town, a dressed-up storefront with a shaker roof and neon lights in the windows flashing *Duffy's* in full color. Jack and Guy entered with an approving nod. They found an oblong oak table with a varnished shine by the window that would hold six men. They pulled out the red-leather chairs and took a seat while they checked out the interior and looked for the advertised girls.

Jack gave a low whistle; "Check out the red-headed doll by the bar," he leaned toward Guy. He waved at her. "Think I'm in love."

Guy gave him a rugged punch in the shoulder. "Cut it out, Donner." Guy had also caught sight of the cute young miss with the long, curly red locks. He gave her a wink as she approached the table with a tablet in hand.

The young men ignored her, eager to hear of adventure. "So, what was it like out there on the sea? Had to be exciting."

"I didn't see much action," Guy said. "I was an airplane mechanic – I only fixed what this guy broke," he pointed at Jack with a playful glare. "But yeah, it was exciting – and scary. The Japs weren't our only enemy. We had a couple of typhoons that almost swept us into the ocean, diseases that spread through the ship, and always the enemy lurking above and below us. We had our share of funerals at sea. This guy," he pointed at Jack, "saw the real action. He was a fighter pilot."

Jo stood at the end of the table tapping her pencil on her notebook, waiting for them to stop talking. Jack noticed her and winked. "At your service, beautiful."

She rolled her eyes. "What can I get you fellas? Wanna try the onion rings? Best in Lincoln."

The young men ordered their food, but were on the edge of their chairs, anxious to hear more. Jack picked up the story.

"Yeah, we have some stories to tell – good, bad, and ugly. Remember the guy who backed right up into the props, Erv? You would think with all the planes on deck, they would've known to watch out for live ones, but that one time...." Jack shuddered at the thought.

Guy nodded as a grimace wrinkled his face. "Didn't realize those props would suck him right in."

"Got way too close – the bloody bastard," continued Jack with a shudder.

"Bastard." The word burned into Guy's brain as Jack prattled on about his love for the Navy. It was the last word he remembered Pa yelling at him as he lay bloodied on the barn floor.

"I couldn't wait to join," Jack said, "but I wasn't even eighteen yet. My dad had to sign for me to get in. The recruiter said to tell my dad goodbye. Asked the recruiter if I'd be leaving that week, and he laughed at me. 'I'm your daddy now, and the bus leaves at six o'clock.' I asked, six o'clock tomorrow morning? And he said, 'No – six o'clock tonight. You have one hour to pack your bags.'" Jack let out a hearty laugh. "I sure had a lot to learn."

Jack's voice faded in the background as Guy's mind flooded back fourteen years to the past he had tried so hard to forget. Bastard. Yeah, he'd heard that word a lot growing up. It's what led to his downfall.

"Ya back already, you bastard?" LeRoy Larue took a swig from the bottle he held close to his bosom. "Thought ya's were with Simmons." He glared at Guy through glassy eyes.

Guy found his father in the barn behind the boarded-up shack, drunk again. He was sprawled over a straw bale – a makeshift bed-stool-chair in the place he now called home. It was no surprise.

"Been there almost three years, Pa. Ran away. Had to talk to you. I have to know why you left us kids all alone outside in the dark, and expected us to sit and wait for you in the cold icy rain?"

He shrugged his shoulders. "Din't know what else ta do." His voice held no emotion.

"So you just left? Never planned to come back?"

"Hard ta 'splain...."

Guy pushed his hand through his coarse black hair in exasperation. "But that wasn't the worst of it, Pa. Then you sold me to Simmons."

"Din't sell ya," Larue frowned. "Had a debt ta pay."

"Admit it, Pa." Guy stuck his finger in his father's chest. "You used me. Used me to pay your debt. All I was to you was property to use and sell."

Larue bobbled his head with neither a yay or nay.

"You never wanted me. All you wanted was for me to be gone."

LeRoy's frown turned into a snarl. "Yore right. 'Cuz yore jest a stupid bastard. Din't want ya's 'cuz yore not my kid anyways." He swore.

Guy stumbled backwards a few steps. "What?! What did you say?"

LeRoy staggered to his feet, his eyes narrow and his mouth tight. "Ya heard me, awright. Yore not my kid. Ah was jest gitting ya's back to yore rightful owner." He laughed at the joke he thought he'd made.

"To Simmons?" All of a sudden it felt hard to breathe; he felt faint at the unbelievable news.

Larue let out a whoop and spit on the floor. "Yore not my kid; yore his."

The words caught Guy off guard. He felt as if in a daze. *Is that why I was treated harsher and given all the chores to do? Not because I was the oldest and most responsible like Ma said? Ma loved me. She told me I was husky and strong – Pa's big helper.*

Guy's mind spun with questions. *Not his kid?* Things started to make sense – the extra chores, the beatings, the lack of any fatherly love.

"Neva' did like ya's," LeRoy slurred. "Yore ma got into bed with Simmons and made a bastard. That's all ya's are: a sad and sorry bastard."

His laugh mocked Guy and made him burn with anger. *I knew he never loved me, but this is too much.* "Don't call me that," Guy warned, ready to duck Pa's reliable swing whenever he was drunk. This time he was mad enough to fight back.

LeRoy staggered to his feet and swung at Guy in drunken fury. "Bastard!"

Guy bobbed and missed the powerful swing. LeRoy lunged forward and tumbled on his face to the barn floor. Enraged, he pulled himself up, grabbed the pitchfork, and jabbed at Guy with all his strength. Guy's eyes widened in horrified realization. Pa didn't only want him gone – he wanted him dead.

"Stop it, Pa! Stop!" He knocked the pitchfork loose from his pa's hand as he swerved to miss another jab. It fell to the floor. Guy bent to pick it up. LeRoy lunged at him from behind. Without thinking, Guy swung around to stop the attack, pitchfork in hand, and struck LeRoy on the head. A huge gash opened; blood gushed down LeRoy's face and onto his shirt.

Surprised and inflamed with drunken rage, the father made another thrust toward the son. Guy let LeRoy stumble forward to the floor, and then struck him in the back with the pitchfork, on purpose this time. As rage overtook his brain, the young man struck the man he'd known all his life as "Pa." Bastard. That's all you are.... He struck him again. Not my kid.... And again until his pa slumped to the floor in a heap.

"Get up and fight, Pa." But his pa didn't move. Blood soaked the man's face and shirt. Guy kicked his father's side. No movement.

He threw down the pitchfork and collapsed onto a straw bale, huffing his breaths. Passed out again, or dead? He wasn't sure.

Guy's breathing slowed as he observed the lifeless body on the floor. *I'm glad Pa's gone. He deserved it.* His mind and heart raced with guilty satisfaction. *But no one can ever know. I have to get away – far, far away.* Guy recklessly put a plan together in his mind, kicked straw on top of the body, and ran from the barn, leaving his jacket behind.

Old enough to join the military, he hitchhiked to Omaha, found the recruiter, and joined the Navy. He would go to sea and fight the enemy. He'd get as far away as possible and hope fate would find him and kill him. That would be best for everyone. His brothers and sisters were better off without him. It would be better if he just disappeared.

"So, what about you? Did you have to get permission too?" one of the guys asked.

Guy's attention was focused on the past, oblivious to everything around him.

"Where are you, champ?" Jack poked him. "They asked if you had to get permission to join, too."

Guy snapped back to the present with a jerk. "Ah...no. I ran away and joined on my own terms."

CHAPTER 6 - THE BOYS AT DUFFY'S

"Refill, boys?" Jo put on a smile with a tilt of her red head. She studied the big guy they called Erv with curiosity. A brute of a man with wavy black hair and dark eyes, there was something about him that gave him mystique. She felt like she should know him. Maybe she'd seen him somewhere? She couldn't place him.

Guy looked at her name badge. "Thanks, Jo. Think I'm calling it quits."

"Not me," Jack interjected. "Bring me another of the same, Babe."

Jo wrinkled her forehead with reservation, but nodded.

Guy noticed her discomfort. "Cut it out, Jack." He frowned at his friend and then apologized for him. "Sorry, miss."

Jo bit her lip and tried to smile. "It's okay. I'll get him another."

"And another order of those great onion rings," called one of the other men.

Guy watched as she walked toward the bar. *Cute kid. My kid sister used to have red curls like hers.* He noticed an older man approach her. There appeared to be an argument as she shook her head and pulled her hand away from his grip. Guy's muscles tensed in an urge to rescue her, but he didn't move. There was something about the girl he felt the need to protect, although he didn't know her. He decided to ask if he could talk with her.

"Hey, bud. Come back to earth. You were out in space again. Where do you go, man?" Guy jumped as Jack gave him a hearty punch in the arm.

"I was telling the guys about the time the tail hook came off my jet. Remember?"

Guy laughed. "That little tail hook is supposed to slow your jet and help it stop, but you must have lost it in combat."

"Don't know. Must have knocked it off somewhere."

"His bomber ran smack-dad into all the docked planes before it stopped and Jack couldn't aim it any other direction. What an explosion! Started several planes on fire, including his. Made Captain Buck a little upset."

"More than a little upset," Jack slapped his knee. "Thought I was headed straight into the ocean."

"You're lucky we got you out in time. You could have been burnt to a crisp."

Jack suddenly turned somber, his quirky grin gone. "Yeah. I know."

"It had to be really scary," said one of the guys. "Bombs exploding and planes shooting at you."

Both men nodded. "We thought we were going to die out there."

"The *Yorktown* sat dead in the water after being bombed twice by the Japs. It was taking on water fast."

"And then it was bombed a third time. Somehow it seemed to right itself again. Tink and I rushed below deck to see if we could fix things," said Guy.

"Something eerie about a dead ship," Jack mused. "All it can do is drift like a ghost ship. Captain Buck told us to prepare to abandon ship. Sailors began to bail by the dozens while bullets bombarded us. Some before getting their life vests on. Yeah. It was real scary." Jack squeezed his eyes closed as he recalled the infamous day. Guy picked up the story.

"Tink and I checked the gaping hole. Engines were beyond repair, and Tink was about to give up. He went to the boiler room. It wasn't more than two minutes when the third bomb dropped. Shrapnel exploded everywhere. Then, I heard Tink scream. I ran and found him with metal in his chest and head. He was out of his mind with pain, said he couldn't see. I moved him to a safer place and ran to find bandages."

"Cap thought everyone had gotten off the ship. He had done a walk-around, and the sea was full of men."

"Were there sharks in the water?"

"Oh, yeah. Not only sharks, but subs below us. Torpedoes, too. Oil and fuel poured into the ocean from our damaged ship, and we gulped that salty-oily mix. Almost drowned us."

"Did ya get rescued?" asked a wide-eyed kid as he slurped his soda.

The men all erupted in laughter.

"Guess you'll have to wait until next time to hear the rest of the story, kid." Guy gave a hearty laugh. "Gettin' late. Gotta work tomorrow."

"Good one, sport. Keep 'em guessin'." Jack hooted as he rose from the table. "Hey, I got this." He swiped the bill. "I'll go pay and see if I can hit it off with little 'Red.'" Jack eyed the waitress and licked his lips.

"Oh, no you don't. This one's mine," Guy grabbed the bill from his hand. "And you leave that one alone," he nodded at the redhead.

Jack shrugged his shoulders. "If you insist. You're a sly one, Larue." He slapped him on the shoulder. "See you tomorrow."

Guy waited until all the guys left the pub, and then took the bill to the bar.

"Ready?" asked Jo.

"Yeah," Guy replied. His look became serious. "Do you have a few minutes?"

Jo squinted, and a frown creased her forehead as she took the money from his hand. "Why?" Her eyes darted back toward the kitchen to see if George had his eye on her.

"Want to ask you a couple questions, if that's okay."

"I can't...I mean, I don't...." Embarrassed, she couldn't find the right words to say. She peered at him, and then at the floor.

"Oh! Whoa! Hold on, Jo," Guy caught her drift. "I only want to talk to you. Nothing more."

He watched her frown release. "Oh, I'm so sorry. I thought you meant...I mean...ooh, I feel so foolish." Jo's face reddened. "It's just that...."

Guy grinned. "Never mind. No problem, Jo. You're a cute kid. I have something to ask you. I'll even wait until the end of your shift if you want."

She nodded with reservation. She sure wished she had a big brother to watch out for her.

C. A. Simonson

CHAPTER 7 - NO STRINGS ATTACHED

Jo finished wiping the last table while she admired the young man who wanted to talk to her. *Could this be a man I don't have to fear? He looks like a gentleman, and he scolded his friend for calling me "Babe."* Her defenses rose on instinct. *Can't be too careful. The men in my life have not been kind.*

Guy looked through the newspaper while he waited. He had told Jack to go on ahead; he would find his own way back to the barracks. The exchange he witnessed earlier between the young waitress and the older man made his skin crawl. He had to know how, or if, he could help.

Jo grabbed a cola and sat down across from him. "Heard the other guys call you Erv."

He nodded with a slight smile. "Thanks for giving me some time. I'll come right to the point. Look, Jo, it's none of my business, but I saw an older man come in earlier to...ah, to talk to you. He seemed to bother and frustrate you – like you didn't want to deal with him."

Jo shifted in her seat and twisted her red curls around her finger. Her face seemed frozen with a strange, fearful look. "Oh. That was John." She tried to sound casual, but her voice quivered. She folded her arms around herself. "He comes here often." She wanted to tell him he was her adoptive father – the man she loathed and feared.

"You don't like John, do you?"

"Is it that obvious? George says I must act more professional, but you are right. I don't like John."

"Well, like I said, it's none of my business, but if you ever need someone to step up and say a few words to this guy," Guy doubled his hand into a fist, "if you know what I mean, I will."

"You would do that for me? You don't even know me – or John." *...or his wrath.*

"Well, I'm smart enough to see a girl in distress."

Jo's face crinkled with worry. "So...," she paused with worried look, "...what's in it for you?" She kept her voice low as she held her breath.

"Nothing. I only want to help you. Would that be okay with you?"

"No strings attached?"

"No strings attached. Promise."

She nodded with reservation. "Okay...I guess."

"Good. You may see me around here more often, then. You live far from here? I could take you home."

With defenses raised again, she shook her head with a squint and then frowned. "I live upstairs," she pointed above the bar.

Guy arched his eyebrows. He knew the kind of women who lived 'upstairs'.

"No— Oh! No!" she caught the unsaid meaning,

"it's not like that. I'm not one of *those* girls. I just work here at Duffy's — I mean, I wait tables here. That's all."

"And how did you come to live here — in this..." he hesitated, not knowing how to phrase it, "... this place? Aren't there better places for a young girl to live?"

Jo stared at the table, ashamed. Yeah, there were lots of better places — McMillans' for one, in their rich estate, but she had hated it there. She thought of the beautiful apartment John had provided. The place was beautiful, fully furnished— and secluded. *And I was all alone....* Her mind drifted.

"Jo?"

"Oh...sorry. Yeah...well," she faltered as she put her words in order, "this was all I could afford. George had the extra room when one of his girls left, so here I am. He said I could live and eat here in exchange for pay."

"No spending money?"

"Tips." She shrugged. "What more does a girl need?" She tried to laugh.

"Well, here's my phone number, in case you ever need help," Guy reached toward her.

She drew back on instinct. He noticed her hesitancy.

"I appreciate it, Erv. But why do you want to help me? What do you really want from me?"

"Absolutely nothing, Jo. Honest."

"No favors?" Her forehead furrowed with suspicion.

"No favors. Trust me."

"Then, why? Why me?"

"You look like a good kid who may have gotten her share of raw deals. Feel like I want to help, that's all. You look like you could use a big brother, nothing more."

Jo breathed in deeply as her shoulders relaxed. She gave him a big smile. "It means a lot to me, Erv. You'll never know how much I need a big brother."

CHAPTER 8 - CALL TO GRACE

Jo held her breath as she dialed the number. She hoped she had made the right decision. *What will Sissie say? Will she even take time to listen?* The phone rang on the other end as Jo waited and bit her lip.

"Grace, can you get that? Probably for you anyway."

"Sure, Mother," Grace giggled. "Just because William calls me all the time?" Grace picked up the phone. "McMillan residence."

"Gracie," Jo breathed a sigh of relief. "I'm so glad you answered. I was afraid it would be Joan — I mean, Mother."

"Josie!" she squealed in delight. "I'm so happy to hear from you! How are you? Are you okay? Is everything all right? It's been so many months."

"Almost a year, and I'm sorry about that. You're not mad at me then?"

"Mad at you? Why would I be mad? I'm getting married! Everything is grand."

Jo rolled her eyes, though Grace couldn't see them. *Always the upbeat, spoiled sister.* "I'm happy for you Sissie. I heard things were getting serious between you and your boyfriend. I worried you'd be mad at me because the last time we spoke, our words got a little heated."

"Oh. You mean our conversation about Father."

"Yes – about John. I refuse to call him anything that has to do with being a father."

"He is our adoptive father. He loves us like his own."

"Oh, sweet Gracie, I wish that were true. Does he treat you well?"

"Of course. Father has always been good to me,."

"Without any expectations?"

"I'm not sure what you mean, but he gives me everything I need," her voice rose with excitement, "including a *big* wedding with everything..."

"...everything you want?" Jo finished her sentence. "Mother sees to that, doesn't she?" She decided to stop drilling for answers, but she couldn't help but snicker as she heard Grace agree with a giggle.

"I wish you could be here. I'm so excited, and I wanted to share my special day with you. I wanted you to be my maid of honor, but Mother said it was too far for you to come home. Do you think you could get away?"

Jo was puzzled. "Where do you think I am?"

"At college, of course, silly. You're at Princeton on the East Coast, pursuing your dream." Grace said it as if she had heard it rehearsed many times.

"Is that what Mother said?"

"Yes."

"And what exactly is my dream?"

"Art, of course. Your major is Medieval Art and you're working hard so you can study in London. Mother says you're planning a trip there soon."

Jo shook her head. *Why the lies?*

"Do you think you can take a break to come home for my wedding in December?"

"Grace," Jo's tone was low. "Let me be clear. I'm not at Princeton. I've never been to the East Coast. I'm not going to London, and I never plan to go. I'm right here in Lincoln and have been for the last year," she spoke slowly and distinctly.

"What? I don't understand," Grace's voice raised a pitch in surprise.

"Listen to me. I need to meet with you and talk face to face. It's not something we should discuss over the phone."

"Sure, Josie," she sounded confused. "But why would Mother say you were away at college? Or that you were going to London?"

"My guess? Maybe she thinks that's where I am. All I know, is John has known all along where I've been. Believe me. He knows I live downtown. I'll tell you all about it when we meet. Not now."

"You could come over to the house."

"No. I can't do that, Sissie."

"Then where? Your place?"

Jo shuddered. *I'd never want Grace to see*

where and how I live. Have to think. "How about Charlotte's Café in downtown Lincoln? Next Thursday, maybe?"

"Where's that?"

"It's a cute little café downtown at 8th and O Streets. Has embroidered curtains in the windows."

"Okay. I'll find it. Can't wait to see you again."

"Me too. And Sissie? I would love nothing better than to be your maid of honor."

CHAPTER 9 - WAR STORIES

"The boys want to hear the end of your story, bud. You up for it?" Jack asked Guy as they headed toward the barracks after work.

"Sure, why not? I'll get cleaned up a bit, and meet you at Duffy's. Six o'clock?"

"Duffy's at six. I'll tell them.

Guy was glad. He wanted an excuse to check on the little redhead again. She was too young to work in a place like Duffy's. For whatever reason – he couldn't put a finger on it – he felt the need to protect her.

The crew sat down at their oblong table by the window and hailed Jo for drinks. She came to take orders. "Jack, isn't it?" she nodded at the young man.

"Will you listen to that, boys? She remembered my name. I'm in heaven."

"...and Erv, if I remember right," she gave him a tilt of her head with a flirty smile.

Guy nodded. He watched the young men as Jo took their orders. They wanted their food, but they were also eager to hear of more adventure.

One of the guys could wait no longer. "Jack promised us more war stories."

Guy snickered. "Okay." He grinned and thought a minute. Here's a good one about Jack when he landed his bomber at night."

"Oh, please, not that embarrassing story...." Jack cut in.

"They want war stories, we'll give them war stories," Guy waved him off.

Jack shook his head and the men laughed.

"Jack hadn't had too much training on night landing."

"In fact, we even had Japs trying to land on our ship, mistaking it for their own. None of the pilots knew how to fly well at night," added Jack.

"The tail hook got caught on something when he landed because he came in much too low."

"It was one of the first times I landed at night," Jack defended.

"That's your excuse," Guy laughed. "He should have killed the engine; instead, he revved it up. It made his jet hop the deck into three other loaded planes. What an explosion! Fires were everywhere!"

"In my defense, the high winds didn't help. That made it harder to land that night, and easier for the fires to spread."

"Quit making excuses, Donner."

"Flames shot over eighty feet in the air, and gas tanks exploded. The fifty calibers got so hot, they exploded too. Talk about fireworks! It was hell! Captain Jocko wasn't too happy with me." Jack smacked his own head.

"Good thing the lieutenant turned on the sprinkler system when he did," Guy commented. "I was an airplane mechanic, but when it came to fires, I was expected to help with fire control too. Everyone did their part."

As Jo refilled their drinks, she heard someone say, "Okay, Erv. Your turn to tell us about your rescue at sea. We're dying to hear about it."

Jo was intrigued too. She had to hear more. She lingered to fill their drinks.

"Yeah," said another. "Jack said everyone abandoned ship except for you. Why?"

"Tink and I never heard the order. We were in the bowels of the ship. The *Yorktown* had been bombed and badly wounded. Three times, bombs ripped through her hull. She fought hard and stayed afloat for over three days. We tried to fix her, but the damage was too great."

"In order to save as many as possible, the Captain called for an abandon ship. She was sinking. Water lapped at the deck, and it seemed hopeless," Jack chimed in.

"But how did you get left behind, Erv?"

"After the first bombs hit, the boilers were damaged. The men in charge of the boilers remained at their posts and maintained enough steam pressure to keep the auxiliary steam systems going as long as they could. We slowed to a stop soon after the attack. The flight deck was repaired enough so planes could take off."

"Then I heard Buck yell out, "Diving attack!" Starboard beam!""

"That meant a Japanese fighter had dropped a bomb on the right front end of the ship," explained Guy to the inquisitive men. They leaned forward to hear every word.

"It ripped a ten-foot hole on the flight deck before it exploded in the lower part of the smokestack. The whole gun crew lay in a heap where the bomb had exploded, one on top of another," Guy paused and shook his head. "It was awful. I didn't want to look, because... because I couldn't recognize any of them. Exhaust gasses rushed toward the deck and stung my eyes. Smoke and flames made it hard to breathe. I rushed below decks to help put fires out with my friend, Tink."

"I asked him if we were going to make it. His answer was, 'Just have faith.'"

Jack picked up the story. "Our ship had been mortally wounded; she lost power and went dead in the water with a jammed rudder and an increasing list to port."

"What's that mean?" asked one of the guys.

"It means the ship was leaning to the left in the water, not upright like it should have been, and falling over more by the minute. It was a bad day for all of us," remembered Jack. "We didn't know it would be our last fight when we woke up that morning. For some, it was their last day on earth.

The ship was dead. Couldn't go anywhere. So Captain Buck told us to get our lifejackets on and get ready to abandon ship. We hurried to the Hammer deck where we could slide down the two-inch ropes. I slid down so fast my hands got rope burn, and sunk almost twelve feet under water. Gulped a bunch of oily ocean water on the way down. The oil mixed with the blood and salt of the ocean made me want to vomit. Sharks were everywhere, and it was a bloody mess, so I tried to drift away from the ship," Jack recalled with a shudder. "It was an awful day."

"Tink and I were below decks when the last bombs fell. Fires burned through several decks which let more water in, but the ship refused to give up and go down. Then Tink got hit. He lay bleeding and broken with shrapnel in his chest and head. I tried to bandage him up and wait for help to come," remembered Guy.

Jo noticed how sad he looked. *How horrible it must have been for them.* She busied herself at the next table to hear more.

"So they left you onboard?" The men's eyes widened as they hung on every word.

"Not on purpose," defended Jack. "Buck thought everyone was off the ship. He had done a search of the ship for any warm bodies, but found no one. The next day someone on a nearby ship heard machine gunfire coming from the ship."

Guy gave a sheepish grin. "That was me. Had to get someone's attention. As much as I thought I wanted to die at sea, that wasn't true when it came right down to it. I wasn't ready. The U.S.S. *Hughes* happened to have patrol in the area and heard the noise. That's when we were rescued."

Guy's smile faded as he recalled the scene. "It was unfortunate for Tink, because he was severely wounded. He almost made it, but died moments before we docked at Pearl Harbor. He had told me to have faith, but my faith was challenged right then and there. Seemed his faith didn't work for him...." Guy's voice trailed.

"Did the ship sink, then?"

"She lasted one more day, and then finally gave up the battle. The ship's still out there in the depths of the South Pacific, not far from Hawaii," said Jack. "She was a magnificent ship."

Guy nodded in somber reflection.

"Best job I ever had," said Jack.

"Me too," admitted Guy. "We were like family."

Jo was awestruck. She had to refill their drinks several times just to hear the incredible story. She was enamored by this amazing young man who volunteered to be her guardian angel and her "big brother." Now, he was also her hero.

CHAPTER 10 - CHARLOTTE'S CAFE

Jo hurried to reach Charlotte's Café by six o'clock after her shift ended at five-thirty. On her way in, she noticed a HELP WANTED sign in the window. She promised herself she would get an application before she left.

She settled into a corner booth in the back of the room, and rearranged the napkins and condiments while she waited for her younger sister. It had been many months since they had seen or spoken to each other. She was anxious and a little worried, but it turned out to be without cause.

Grace seemed to float in on a cloud, all smiles. She searched the café for Jo. They spotted each other, and Jo got up and went to greet her with a hug.

"Grace, you look radiant," Jo smiled as she wrapped her arms around her sister. "I'm glad you came."

"What a big surprise!" She squeezed her. "I'm so happy to see you! Wish I would have known. You were in town all this time? You could've helped me plan my wedding! I have so many questions...." Her voice betrayed the confusion written on her face.

"I'm thrilled to see you again too! Looks like

you're doing well. You're radiant!" She pulled her in close for a tight squeeze. "We'll talk, I promise. I have a lot to tell you."

Grace's face turned to concern as she cupped Jo's face in her hands. "You look tired Jo."

"I've been working hard, Sissie."

"You wouldn't have to work a day in your life, you know that. Father would see to that."

"Most likely he would," Jo said with sarcasm. "Let's not talk about him now."

"Why would Mother tell me you were at college when you were right here in town all this time?" She plopped down into the booth.

Jo's laughter held scorn. "Maybe she thought I needed my space. Maybe she thought I was a bad influence." She shrugged.

"Why would she lie to me? I don't understand. Mother said you were doing well at college, getting ready for a big trip...."

"Lies. All lies. I left to get away from them, and for...ah...other reasons. Someday, maybe I can tell you more—" her voice trailed, "But, not today. Today is a special day. I ordered us both Reubens. Hope that's all right with you?"

"Only if they come with double fries and a chocolate malted!" Grace giggled.

Jo laughed with her. "Tell me about your wedding and about William. How did you meet? What's he like, Sissie?"

"He's a dream, and handsome and sweet and—"

she rolled her eyes and grinned, "and a very hard worker. He might be able to get a job at Father's business. Both Mother and Father fully approve of him."

I'll bet they do, thought Jo.

Grace went on to explain how she and William had met in a park, how they'd fallen in love, and how crazy she was about him.

"How's Mother going to handle losing her baby girl?"

Grace giggled. "She wants us to move into the estate. That's not going to happen," she made a silly face. "But, seriously, she'll be fine – in time. "What about you? Do you have a guy?"

Jo's mind rushed through all the guys she'd had. "No. No one right now...." She thought of her encounter with the black-haired sailor from the bar. "But," she paused, "there may be a prospect." Her eyes twinkled as a sly smirk played across her lips.

"Tell me!"

"Tall, dark, and handsome." Jo stuffed a couple of fries into her mouth and winked.

They laughed. "Jo! What's he really like?"

"He's very kind – not like some of the yahoos I've met. He seems thoughtful and caring."

"Where did you meet him?"

Jo looked at the ceiling to find an answer. "Oh... around. I hope to find out more about him. We're supposed to get together soon."

"Like a date – with a real sailor?"

"Hmmm...something like that."

"That's exciting!" She sipped up the last of her malted.

"Grace?"

"Yeah?"

"Do you ever think about Dolly?"

"No, guess not. Why?"

"I saw a lady the other day who looked like Dolly. Made me lonesome for her. She's been in my thoughts a lot. It would be great if we could find her. She'd love to be a part of your wedding."

"Wouldn't that be swell?" Grace's eyes lit up. "But how would we even go about it?" She dug in her purse to leave a tip.

"Maybe I could give the orphanage a call," Jo thought aloud as they got up to leave.

On the way out the door, Jo grabbed an application with new hope in her heart. There just may be a new future for her on the horizon.

CHAPTER 11 - CONCERN FOR JO

Over the next few weeks, Guy kept a watchful eye over Jo. He didn't see John come into the bar, and she said she hadn't seen him either.

Late one Friday afternoon, Guy entered Duffy's and gave Jo a wave. She waved back, and had his drink ready when he sat down at his usual place at the bar.

"How ya doin', Jo?" he asked. "Been okay?"

"Sure. No problems at all. Work, as usual." She pulled her hair into a ponytail and fastened it with a rubber band. She washed her hands, and then went about her work.

He watched as she served a few people, and then wiped up the bar. "Hey, Jo. Do you ever want to work in a more, ah, family-friendly place – away from here, I mean?"

"Well, sure. Someday – when I can afford to move, or...." She put her finger to her chin as she thought about her options and recent application.

"Jo," called George. "Someone's here to see you." He pointed to a corner table. John stared her way as he drummed the table with his fingers.

"He's here," she whispered to Guy. "That's John. Sorry. Gotta talk to him. He gets mean if I don't."

Guy eyeballed the tall, middle-aged man with a slight tinge of gray in his hair. He looked like some sort of businessman in his pinstriped blue suit and tie. With glassy eyes, the man ogled Jo as she approached him. If Guy hadn't known better, he would have sworn the man was already half-drunk, even though it was only five o'clock in the afternoon.

When Jo neared his table, John grabbed her by the waist and pulled her in.

"John," she scowled at him. She controlled her voice and kept it low. "Stop." She tried to pull herself away, but he held on.

"Whazza matter, baby girl?" he slurred. "Din't ja miss me?"

"John," she spoke louder. "Stop. Now." Jo struggled against his grasp, but he only tightened his grip and pulled her down onto his lap.

Guy's fury rose as he witnessed the scene. The veins in his head swelled. He began to rise from his stool, but questioned whether he should intervene. He stayed seated, but his knuckles turned white as his hands tightened into fists.

"C'mon, Josie," John pleaded like a small boy, "Give your daddy some sugar."

Guy stopped short. *Josie? Her daddy? What's going on here? Had he heard right?*

"You're drunk, John. Now stop!" Her pleading eyes caught Guy's. With all her strength, Jo pried John's arm from around her waist. "Now what do you want?" She tried to be stern as she scooted away from him.

He reached toward her again. "You *know* what I want, darlin'." He rose from the table and grabbed at her. Chairs tipped over as he reached for something to steady his balance.

Guy had had enough. In four steps, he was between Jo and John. "You should leave." He put his hand on John's chest and bore a hole into his face with his eyes.

John stepped back, confused. "Who are you? And why should I care? Jo! Get over here!" He pushed back at Guy.

Guy planted his 160-pound frame and stood his ground. He continued to stare down at the older man. He nodded toward the door and pointed.

George rushed to the scene. "Like he said – you should leave. There'll be no brawl in this bar."

"'s not over, Jo," John warned with his fist. "I'll be back later to get my sugar. Be ready."

Guy noticed Jo's sad eyes as she hung her head and watched John McMillan leave the bar. She shook her head in despair and dared to look at Guy. "Thank you," she mouthed in silence.

"Come here. Sit down a minute." He took her hand and led her across the room. "Talk to me. Tell me what's going on."

Jo looked at her boss, watching her every move, and then at the clock on the wall. "Have to work. Can't."

"It's not that busy in here. Almost quittin' time anyway."

She checked the clock again and let out a sigh. "Give me time to finish up, okay?"

He nodded, pulled up a chair, and grabbed the newspaper to look through as he waited for Jo to finish work. At five-thirty, she sat down across from him and let out a long sigh. Her shoulders wilted as she put her head in her hands. She tried to corral her jumbled thoughts and emotions. Guy wasn't sure if she were in tears or deep in thought, so he remained quiet until she was ready to speak.

Finally, Jo looked up at him. She flushed when she realized he was watching her, but she saw in his black eyes a compassion and empathy, not pity or scorn. She sensed a soft, tender heart and a trustworthy spirit. Otherwise, why would he even care? He had to be ten years her senior. She took the rubber band out of her ponytail, pulled her fingers through her hair, and sighed again as she leaned back in her chair.

"Thanks. It means a lot to me for you to have stepped in like that and stand up for me. I am so tired of this mess. I need to stop him, but I don't know how. What am I going to do?"

"Tell me, Jo. Who is this John? What's his story, and why did he say he's your daddy?"

She breathed heavily. "Long story."

"I'm here to listen, kid." Guy wasn't sure why he even wanted to know, but somehow it felt right.

This girl needed his protection. He wasn't sure why he felt compelled to protect her, he just did.

"John is my adoptive father. My sister and I were adopted by him and his wife, Joan when I was six."

"Pardon me for saying so, but he acted as if he wanted a whole lot more than just a friendly father-daughter talk."

Jo hung her head as the tears slipped from her eyes. "He did."

"Tell me your story. I'd like to hear it. You can trust me. It won't go any further than my ears, I promise."

Jo looked into his soft eyes and knew in her heart he was telling the truth.

C. A. Simonson

CHAPTER 12 - QUESTIONS

"Mother, how could you?" Grace threw her purse on the table in a huff as she stormed into the kitchen.

"Grace, dear, what on earth are you talking about?" Joan was surprised at her daughter's tone and actions.

Grace's usual bubbly, happy demeanor was gone, her tone accusatory. "You told me Josie was at Princeton, going to college – that she was busy preparing for a trip to London. That was the reason you gave me for her not coming to my wedding. Isn't that what you said?"

"Hmmm..." Joan murmured as she twisted her gold cross necklace and nodded, "That's right, honey. Jo is on the East Coast."

"She *is* still there, correct?" She stared her mother in the eye. "In Virginia?"

"New Jersey." Joan corrected, but her brow furrowed as she cocked her head. "Uh...Jo left to go to Princeton last year." Her face flushed at the lie; she could not look at Grace.

"Can we call her? At Princeton, I mean."

"Uh...no. I think she's already in London...." Her hand trembled as she poured herself a glass of wine. "I told you this before, Grace. Jo is too far away to come home right now, or for your wedding in December."

Grace narrowed her eyes and shook her head. "Mother, a bold-faced lie? Straight to my face? Why?"

"No. No, Grace," she stammered. She took a sip of wine and stared at the table. "Why are you asking me about Jo?"

Joan nervously ran her finger around the rim of her glass, and took another drink. She could not look her daughter in the eye.

Grace leaned on the table so that she was face to face with her mother. "You honestly believe Jo is at college?" She frowned.

"Yes, Grace...." Joan stumbled with her words as she searched the ceiling for the appropriate words to say. "Jo left last year to go to Princeton, and...."

"Mother. Stop! Stop lying right now!" Grace shook her head in disgust. "Would it surprise you to know I had supper with Jo last night?"

Joan's eyes widened in fear and her jaw dropped. "What? She's home?"

"Really, Mother?" Grace's anger rose. "You didn't know she was in Lincoln?"

Joan held the wine glass with both hands and took a gulp of wine. Her worried face gave her away. "So, she's really here in Lincoln?"

"Yes, and she's been here all along. She never went to college, never went to the East Coast, and never planned a trip to London," she spat the words. "We ate together last night at Charlotte's Café. She's been living downtown. Why have you lied to me? Why didn't you tell me she was in Lincoln this whole past year?" Grace screeched a chair across the hardwood floor and parked herself in front of Joan. "Why have you lied to me?"

"Uh...you have to....understand. Your father thought it best...."

"Best?" She cut her off. "I don't understand, Mother."

Joan's shoulders slumped. "I may as well tell you the truth since you've already talked to Jo." Joan patted Grace's hand, "Honey, I'm sorry. Yes. I knew Jo wasn't on the East Coast, but honest to God, I didn't know where she was. That's the truth. I thought she had run away again, or had moved in with some of her friends. They aren't a good influence, Grace. We thought it best to let you think she was doing well – away in college."

"Does Father know where she is?" Grace probed although she already knew the answer.

"I think so...." Joan's voice disappeared as she wilted like a shriveled flower in her chair. She looked weary. All she could do is shake her head with an "I-don't-know" look on her face.

Grace bit her lip. She began to understand why her mother led such a lonely life. Things started to make sense, and she wondered whether the things Jo had said about their adoptive father were really true.

CHAPTER 13 - OFFICE VISIT

"Joan, what are you doing here in the middle of the day?" John asked as he looked up from his paper-strewn desk.

Joan closed his office door, and meekly lowered herself into one of the leather chairs in front of his desk.

"We have to talk." Her small voice wavered as she smoothed her skirt of imaginary wrinkles.

"That usually means you need more money," he sighed and leaned to the side to retrieve his wallet. "Did Grace run the bill to the moon and back at the bridal shop? She has her own account, you know. You don't have to pamper her with more."

"No. That's not what we need to talk about. It's Josephine."

John's eyes narrowed. "What about her?"

"You know what I'm talking about. We've never really discussed what happened when she left home last time."

John raised his eyebrows and stared at his wife without emotion. He waited for her to continue.

She mechanically reached for the gold cross on her necklace and began to rub it between her fingers as if it would bring some type of protection or luck. John wouldn't be happy with her for broaching this forbidden topic, but it had to be discussed. She crossed her legs and leaned forward. "We agreed to let Grace think she was away at college."

He stared and nodded without comment.

"You made her leave our home. Why?"

"I didn't make her do anything. It was her choice to leave."

"You forced her out."

"No. I was more than generous to supply her with a fully furnished apartment downtown, a limitless bank account, and a car, but she chose to throw it back in my face."

"And now she's out there all alone. We need to find her and ask her to come back home."

"It wouldn't do any good. She wants her own way."

"Have you tried to call her? To find her?"

His stare was cold. "No," he lied. "She's on her own and that's the way she wants it." His face held no emotion as he shuffled the papers on his desk.

"She needs our help. She needs to come home...." Joan pleaded with her eyes, although she knew it wouldn't help.

He scowled and ignored her.

"Please, John? For Grace?" She wrung her hands.

"Leave it alone, Joan." John's tone was as harsh.

She pouted. "But Grace wants Jo to be in her

wedding."

"It's done, Joan. Let Jo go. You have Grace." Icicles clung to his words.

Frustrated and hurt, Joan stood to her feet, and started toward the door with her head down. With one last feeble attempt, she turned to face him again. "Grace ate dinner with Jo last night at Charlotte's Café. She already knows Jo isn't at college. She knows we've lied," she spoke so quietly, John had to strain to hear.

He looked up with a hint of alarm in his face; he kept his voice steady. "Goodbye, Joan. We'll not speak of this again."

She squeezed her eyes tight and bit her lip to forbid the tears that were bursting in her heart as she hurried out the door. She would not let him see her cry.

John McMillan sat down behind his large oak desk. He restacked the piles of papers and rearranged the gold-framed 11 x 17 picture of Jo on his desk. Not Joan, nor anyone else, could ever know why Jo really left home and preferred not to live in the apartment he provided for her. *If Grace knows she's in town and can contact her, that may be a bigger predicament. I will have to deal with Jo – and soon.*

C. A. Simonson

CHAPTER 14 - JO'S STORY

"Tell me your story, Jo. I sure would like to know you better," Guy's voice was soft and reassuring.

Jo searched his eyes, enamored by his look, his deep voice, and his kind face. She sensed he told the truth; there were no underlying motives. Still, she hesitated. *Can I trust him? Will he betray me too?* She wondered. She decided to take the plunge and tell him everything. She would trust this man who offered to be her guardian angel.

"I hate John." Her face paled at the blunt admission. "I know he's my adoptive father and I should respect him, but from the first day we left the orphanage, he warned me I'd better do as he said or he'd hurt my little sister. I was scared. My older sister was left behind and couldn't protect me anymore. So, I did whatever he wanted. *Whatever* he wanted," she emphasized. "He's never deserved respect." Jo drew in a long breath and closed her eyes as she awaited his response.

"What about your mother? Didn't she have anything to say about it?"

"No. She was clueless, and I was too afraid to tell. I ran away when I was twelve, but didn't get far. John's an important and influential businessman, so he had people everywhere on the lookout for me. I didn't even make it downtown. After that, they gave me my own bedroom. Mother thought if I had my own room, it would solve everything; she thought I had run away because I didn't want to share a room with my sister. She didn't know the real reason – that John wanted me to have a room all to myself where he could come and...ah...." *I can't do this.*

Her body shook. She put her head in her hands and sobbed. Her shoulders heaved with every breath.

"You don't have to tell me. Really. It's none of my business." Guy dug his handkerchief from his pocket and handed it to her. She wiped her eyes and then blew her nose with a loud honk. He sat quietly and waited for her to continue.

"I'm sorry," Jo caught her breath and apologized after a few awkward moments. She gazed at the handsome young man who sat patiently listening.

"I really shouldn't tell you all this. I don't even know you. You just seem like someone I can trust."

"That's okay, Jo," Guy cleared his throat. He reached out to touch her, but drew back. He felt uncomfortable. He had thought he wanted to know, but had he really? He wanted to comfort her, hold her, and say it would be different now that he was around, but he didn't know if that were true.

"You don't have to explain any more. I get the picture. Uh...," he pondered how he should ask,"...is that why he came here today?"

She nodded and hung her head. Her face flushed. "I hate that man." Her mouth tightened, her scorn apparent in her scowl.

"I heard him say he'd be back. Does he know you live upstairs?"

She sighed heavily and closed her eyes. "Yeah. He found me here a few months ago. When I was in high school, I made excuses to be away as much as possible, and then after graduation last year, I left for good. Couldn't stand to live in that house any longer. Like I said, John is powerful in this town, a prominent businessman who knows how to get his way. He didn't want it to appear like he didn't have a good family. So he gave me a beautiful apartment uptown – furnished and everything. Even gave me a bank account and a car. It was real grand, but I knew in my heart the real reason he wanted me there. It was just a trap and a bribe. He wanted me all to himself any time he desired. It was like a prison." Jo hung her head and stared at an invisible spot on the table. Subconsciously, she took a napkin and began to rub at it. "I didn't know what to do."

"What about your sister?"

"She lives in her own world and is oblivious to anyone else. She's Mother's pet. She gets everything she wants. Her life is the total opposite of mine. John and his wife went to the orphanage to adopt one girl. Joan wanted my little sister from the moment she saw her. The orphanage refused to separate us since we were so close in age, so the McMillans were forced to adopt us both. I believe John had other plans for me from the start."

"How did you end up here at Duffy's?"

"I told John I wanted nothing to do with the apartment or anything else he had to offer. Words got heated. So one day, I decided to leave. I knew people, and many offered me places to stay after I left the apartment. I was a little wild in school." Her face reddened in embarrassment. "I moved around a while, from one place to the next, but I really wanted to earn my own way. One of my friends told me they needed waitresses at Duffy's. Well, what he said was "they need girls." Figured I could at least check on it. Told George up front I would wait tables, clean, and even cook if he wanted, I just wouldn't be one of his "girls." Must have taken pity on me, because he agreed. Then, when one of the girls left, a room opened up. It was my chance to be out on my own, and I took it."

"And John found you."

She nodded; she couldn't look at him. "How was I to know he was one of Duffy's loyal customers?"

"It isn't right, Jo. You've got to get away from him —away from here. Give me some time to think things through. I'm sure we can come up with something."

Jo let out another big sigh and dabbed her eyes.

"Thank you. You don't know how much that means to me. I already have a job lead at a little café, so I may be out of here soon. You're more than a guardian angel, you are almost like a big brother."

He smiled, glad to be able to help. He couldn't resist asking the question that gnawed at him. "Jo, the man called you Josie."

Jo tilted her head and wound a curl around her finger. "Yeah. My childhood nickname. My full name is Josephine, but my family called me Josie. Just go by Jo now."

"Curious. I used to have a little sister named Josie. Seems like ages ago," Guy scratched his chin in thought. "She had red curls like yours. Bet she would be about your age, too." He laughed as a small shiver ran up his spine. *Dolly used to curl her hair around her finger the same way.* "Small world. Maybe that's why I felt you needed a big brother."

"What a coincidence," she tilted her head sideways as she studied his face more closely. *Rugged square jaw with defined features, fierce black eyes, and wavy black hair.* "I had a big brother a long time ago. Don't know what happened to him, but I'd bet he'd be a lot like you. At least, I'd hope he would be." She gave him a sweet smile.

"What was his name?"

"Guy."

Guy choked as he gulped down the hard lump

that stuck in his throat. Realization hit him square in the heart. *My little sister Josie... sitting right here ...in front of me...after all these years.* His heart was filled with sudden remorse for not being there for her, and his eyes brimmed at the thought of the horrendous burdens she'd had to bear growing up. A new brotherly love overwhelmed his heart. He was fixated on her face, frozen in thought.

"Something I said?" Jo stared back with curiosity. "Your face is white. Do you feel all right? What's wrong?"

"Jo – or should I call you Josie?" he stammered. "I told you I ran away once too, a long time ago. Felt like I had to get far away from everyone I knew and loved. Joined the Navy and hoped to forget my old life and start a new one. I went by my first name, Ervin, so no one could find me...." He hesitated. He looked at the ceiling and then closed his eyes and inhaled deeply to regain his composure.

She nodded with concern and leaned in to listen, and put her hand gently on his arm. "Yes, please go on."

He paused, swallowed hard, and gazed at her in a whole new way. "My close friends and my family..." he cleared his throat again. Hot tears moistened his eyes, "my brothers and sisters..." he choked out the words, "...knew me by my middle name...."

She waited. Curious. Wondering.

He inhaled another deep breath and let it out slowly. "Josie. I...am...Guy."

Jo's mouth dropped open; her eyes got large.

"I'm your big brother. Ervin Guy Larue."

C. A. Simonson

CHAPTER 15 - BIG BROTHER

Jo's eyes popped with surprise as she put her hand to her mouth. "Guy?" She drew her head back to get a better look. "Is it really you?" She blinked as if in a dream. "I never thought I'd see any of my brothers again." She dabbed at her eyes as they brimmed anew with tears.

"Josie, you're all grown up!" Guy whistled. "Unbelievable. How old are you now?"

"I just turned twenty," she whispered.

Guy shook his head. "Fourteen years since I last saw you. No wonder I didn't recognize you, but you still have all those beautiful red curls. Maybe that's what drew me to you in the first place."

"Where have you been all this time?"

"Long story. The last few years, I've been on a ship in the South Pacific. You probably heard us talking about it."

She nodded as her eyes lingered on her long-lost, but now-found brother.

"Tell me about Gracie. You said you both were adopted together? Does she still live with your adoptive parents?"

"Yes, for now. Grace loves it there. Why wouldn't she? Gets everything and anything her little heart desires and Joan adores her."

"Sounds like a bit of rivalry." He winked. "Do you worry about her? I mean with John and all?"

Jo wrinkled her forehead as she thought. "Grace and I were close when we were at the orphanage; we looked out for each other. But after we were adopted, we grew apart. Grace was so excited to be adopted and to have a new mama and daddy. I didn't want to go from the start, especially when I found out that last day Dolly wasn't coming with us. I threw a grand fit. The administrator pushed me back toward the car and then John picked me up and forced me into the backseat. Said I'd better do what he wanted or he'd hurt Grace. I was afraid and believed him. I cried all the way to their home."

"Do you think John would have hurt Grace, or was it just a threat?"

"I don't know. When you're little, you believe everything people tell you. I was only six years old. As an adult, you want to believe people too, but as you get older and wiser, you learn to distrust everyone because no one tells the truth."

Guy watched her face harden with hurt and his heart went out to her. "I'll always tell you the truth, Jo."

She softened. "I know you will. I trust you. Grace could never understand why I hated living there, and I never told her. She said, 'Just do whatever Father wants, and it'll be fine'. She didn't know what she was asking."

"Do you ever see her?"

"I saw her the other day. She had been told I was away at college and that was why I haven't contacted her this past year."

"They told her that?"

Jo nodded. "Grace was puzzled about why they would lie, but it hasn't dampened her spirits about her wedding. She's getting married, so she'll be gone from that household soon enough. I'm glad. She was happy to know I'm in town because she wants me to be her maid of honor."

They sat in silence for a few moments, each absorbed in thought, studying one another.

"Jo, you said Dolly was at the orphanage too?" She nodded.

"How long ago?"

"We went to the orphanage almost right after all of us left the barn. You told Dolly to take Grace and me to the preacher's, remember? You took the little boys to the Johnsons and Frankie walked to the farmer's down the road."

"Yes, I remember that day well. Tore my gut apart."

"Well, Dolly did take us to the preacher's, and they kept us for a few days. They tried to find a family who would take us in. They couldn't find anyone, so they took us to Overbrook Orphanage. We were there only a couple months when the McMillans came to look for a little girl. I overheard the administrator say they had to keep the sisters together."

"But not Dolly?"

"I thought Miss Smarkel meant all three of us – including Dolly – but she hadn't meant that at all. I didn't know until the day the McMillans came to get us. I discovered later the McMillans never knew there was an older sister. I was so angry, I wanted to run away." She thought a minute. "In fact, I did run away – a few times."

"Have you tried to find Dolly?"

Jo shook her head with a shrug of her shoulders. "Guess I've been wound up in my own world too."

"Maybe you should. You..." Guy paused. "I mean, we, might find Dolly too, if we try." He studied Jo a few minutes, still in awe that he had found his sister. "Do you think I could see Grace? I would really like to, but would she even remember me?"

"She was four when we left home, and you were always gone – working, doing chores or something, somewhere. Don't remember that you were around much, so she may not remember you at all."

"Nevertheless, if you could arrange a time for me to see her, I would love being with real family again," he reached over and squeezed her hand.

"You're right, Guy." Jo's eyes brimmed again. "It would be wonderful to have our whole family back together again."

CHAPTER 16 - THE CALL

"Overbrook Orphanage. How may I direct your call?"

"Yes. Hello. May I speak to the Administrator?"

"Miss Smarkel? I'll see if she's in. What is the nature of your call, miss?"

Jo cleared her throat. Miss Smarkel was still there, after all these years. She could see the image of the old spinster in her mind's eye: tall and skinny, clothes hanging on her, hair piled high in a straw-and-string bird's nest with a pencil poked through the middle to hold it in place. Jo swallowed hard. She could imagine Miss Smarkel squinting over the top of her pop bottle glasses perched on her pointy nose. Miss Smarkel had looked scary to her when she lived there. She not only looked scary, but she *was* scary – and mean. Jo never did like or trust her. *Had she changed?*

"Miss? Are you still there? What would you like to speak to Miss Smarkel about?"

Jo took a deep breath and let it out slowly. "I'm sorry. Lost in thought, I guess. I lived at the orphanage with my sisters when I was a small child. I need information about my sister."

"I see. Your name?"

"Josephine Larue."

No response. Jo waited, but heard only the sounds of breathing. After a long silence, she thought she heard papers being shuffled.

"Well, miss," the lady finally responded, "Our policy states we cannot give out adoptees' information. Therefore, I am not allowed to give you the name of the family who adopted your sister, Grace."

"No, Ma'am. You misunderstood. Grace and I were adopted together. I already know who adopted us."

"That is strange, Miss Larue. Our records show one Larue was adopted: a Grace Larue."

Jo frowned. *Then Dolly was not adopted?* "I'm confused, ma'am. I called about my older sister, Dolly Larue. I need to find her. Perhaps Miss Smarkel will remember. May I speak with her?"

Silence again. Perhaps she was putting the call through. Jo crossed and then uncrossed her legs, stood up, sat down, and stood up again. Her nerves were in tatters. *Why was it taking so long? Maybe this call hadn't been such a good idea after all.* She almost hung up the phone when a familiar, squeaky voice answered.

"Hel-loooo. This is Marva Smarkel."

A chill went up Jo's back. All her memories of the squeaky-voiced administrator flooded back. "Um, hello, Miss Smarkel? This is Josephine La...ah...Mc...McMillan," Jo stammered, frightened anew at the remembrance of the scary administrator who had once pushed her into John McMillan's arms.

Silence. Miss Smarkel waited for her to continue. Seconds that felt like minutes ticked away.

"Ah...you may remember me as Josie Larue."

A few more seconds of silence until the shrill voice asked, "And you said you lived at Overbrook? When?"

"Um..." she calculated in her head, "... about fourteen years ago; I was six years old when my sisters and I arrived at the home."

"That's a while back, Miss Larue. My memory isn't as good as it used to be."

"My little sister Grace, and I were adopted soon after we came to Overbrook. We were there for two months when Mr. and Mrs. John McMillan from Lincoln adopted us." Jo twisted her curls around her fingers while she awaited the lady's response. Her nerves were on edge. All she heard was breathing and the tapping of a pencil on the other end of the phone.

"Uh, I called because I want to locate my older sister, Dolly. She came with us to the orphanage. Do you remember us?" She heard the administrator clear her throat a few times. "Please, Miss Smarkel. It would mean an awful lot to me to find Dolly. Please answer me. Are you there?"

Finally, the lady spoke. Her tone was formal, calculated. "Yes, Miss Larue – or do you go by Miss

McMillan now? I am here. And I do remember you and your little sister, Grace. It was a rough day for you when the McMillans came to get you. I do remember. You didn't want to go with them that day, if I remember correctly."

"Yes, ma'am. I didn't want to leave without telling Dolly where we were going. I wanted to at least say goodbye, and you wouldn't let me." Jo's anger and frustration resurfaced at the remembrance.

Miss Smarkel detected Jo's bitterness, but maintained her composure. She steadied her voice before she answered. "Yes, I remember, and I'm sorry. It was, and still is the policy here at Overbrook to not give out any personal information. If siblings are separated, their locations must be held in strictest confidence for the sake of the adoptive parents, especially if the birth parents are still alive. We understood your birth father may still be a threat. Dolly wasn't told where the two of you went or who adopted you either. I am sorry, but that is just how it is."

Something sounds fishy. With new resilience, she pressed. "I am her sister, not her parent. I have to find her. Can't you tell me now? It's been over a decade, Miss Smarkel."

There was a short silence. "Well...." Miss Smarkel paused a few seconds. "It *has* been over ten years now, hasn't it? Hold on while I look up her file."

Marva Smarkel didn't have to look up any file. She remembered Dolly Larue inside and out. Now a successful businesswoman in her own right, Dolores Larue Ryan owned her own sewing company and made or mended most of the uniforms for the orphanage. Marva Smarkel had helped her get that start many years ago when she placed Dolly as an apprentice with Violet Hendricks, a successful seamstress in Fremont. She stalled for time on how to approach this predicament. She had hoped this moment would never arrive.

Jo bit her nails and waited. Her skin prickled with anticipation. Her hope piqued. Maybe she was really going to find Dolly.

"Miss McMillan? Your sister Dolores, or Dolly as you called her, went to live in Fremont, Nebraska, in January 1937, only a month after you and Grace moved in with the McMillans."

Jo could barely contain her excitement as she clung to the telephone. "Do you have her phone number?"

"Sorry, Miss McMillan," the Administrator lied, "that is all I have to give. I may have bent the rules too much by giving you what I did."

Jo's heart sank. "It's enough. Thank you so much, Miss Smarkel."

"If I may ask, has it been a good experience for you with the McMillans?" Miss Smarkel remembered the well-to-do couple who gave the orphanage a hefty donation after the adoption of both girls, with the caveat to keep Josesphine's name off the papers. John McMillan continued to send money to Overbrook as a contingency to keep mouths silent.

It was Jo's turn to be silent a few moments as she thought how she should answer the woman. "They have provided for us well," she finally said. "Grace has thrived there."

"And you?"

Jo avoided the question. "Thank you for your help, Miss Smarkel. It means a lot to me. Goodbye." She hung up the phone before the administrator could ask anything more. She was excited to have some real information on Dolly and at least a lead to follow. But it niggled in her craw why the receptionist told her only Grace had been adopted.

Why is there nothing on me?

CHAPTER 17 - A DAY IN LINCOLN

Dol and Ben enjoyed lively chitchat and simply being a couple again on the hour long drive to Lincoln. It had been a long time since they had had alone-time with three children underfoot and Dol's home sewing business to keep her busy.

"What do you suppose Simmons wants from you? Surely, he can't think you'll give him a 'get-out-of-jail-free' card."

"No. He knows he's in there for several years on the manslaughter charge. It's curious. It seemed urgent for him to contact me. Guess I'll know soon enough."

Dol changed the subject. "Frank called me the other day. He was quite concerned about Guy."

"You said it looked like Guy had changed his name, and Frank had to do some digging to find him."

"Yeah. We figure it has to be Guy, because he's the only Larue from Tekamah, Nebraska."

"Strange. Did he find which ship Guy was on?"

"Yes, he did, and that's what worries him – and me. Guy may have been assigned to the *Yorktown* – the one that sunk during battle."

Ben let out a whistle. "Whew. Any survivors?"

"Some – but Frank doesn't know if Guy was one of them. He's still checking."

They sat in silence a few minutes as they thought of the ramifications and if they would ever see Guy again.

"Oh, yeah. Frank had more news too. Told me he became a minister – a real reverend, can you believe it? Official license and the whole works."

"Now that's hard to believe," he grinned. "Your brother Frank, a minister. Hmmm. But then he was doing a lot of church work up there. Suppose it figures for him to go into it fulltime. Did he ever marry the girl he liked in Wisconsin? Anne, wasn't it?"

"Um-hmm, her name was Anne. I don't think he married her – at least we weren't invited to any wedding," she joked. "Frank said she wanted to finish college first, so he is biding his time. Jenna hoped Frank would fall for her. I did too, for Jenna's sake – and mine, if I were honest. God must have someone else picked out for my best friend Jenna. Anne was Frank's first love. Give him time."

"He'll end up a bachelor if he waits too long," Ben chuckled. "All the best gals will be taken."

As they passed a WELCOME TO LINCOLN sign, Ben and Dol made arrangements on when and where to meet later. He dropped her off downtown to shop to her heart's content while he

headed southwest to the Nebraska State
Penitentiary to meet with Mr. Sy Simmons.

"I'll be back around four o'clock to pick you up,
Sweets."

Dol was excited to shop without having three
children in tow. She had new fabrics and trims to
select for her sewing business and Christmas
presents to purchase for the kids. There were so
many stores and such huge selections, she was in
her glory; Dol loved to shop. After a couple of
hours, she had an armload of packages and bags.
Her feet were swollen, she was tired, and ready to
sit down.

She found a quaint little café that looked like a
great place for an afternoon coffee break. She went
inside and found a small table by the window. She
examined the charming embroidered curtains in
the window. It pleased her to see the craftsmanship
in design. The waitress approached as she fondled
the fabric between her fingers.

"Hi, I'm Jo. Coffee?" She gave her a sweet
smile.

"Coffee sounds wonderful. Cream and sugar,
please. It's a pleasure to have good coffee again
after all this ration nonsense," she smiled back.

Jo nodded and went to get the beverage.
*Something curious about this woman. Her smile
reminds me of Dolly, but I won't embarrass myself
and stare at her like I did at the woman a couple*

weeks ago at the bar. She shook herself of the thoughts.

"May I recommend a piece of pie this afternoon? Charlotte's is known for the best cherry and peach pies in the area," Jo set the coffee before the lady. "And even though sugar is still rationed, our bakers know how to make our desserts sweet."

"Hmmm, sounds good. Which one would you recommend? I can't decide." Dol curled an unruly wisp of blond hair around her finger as she contemplated and looked at the pictures in the menu. Jo cocked her head. *Where have I heard that voice before?*

"I love the peach pie here. It's especially good with ice cream on top," she recommended.

"Then peach it is," Dol replied with a warm smile, "and make it à la mode."

Jo observed the lady, trying her best to place the voice that sounded so familiar, the smile, and the mannerisms. *My mind's playing tricks on me again.* She shook her head again to shake the uncanny feeling and dismissed the pesky thoughts swarming in her head.

Dol finished her pie, left a big tip, and rose to pay the bill. "Thank you, miss. The pie was glorious."

On her way out the door, an outraged older man bumped roughly into her and almost knocked her down. Her packages tumbled to the floor and purse contents spilled everywhere.

"Look where you're going, lady," he growled.

Dol glared into his angry eyes with faint recognition. She knelt to pick up her belongings and saw him march up to the waitress with blatant determination. The girl looked worried. Dol couldn't be positive, but somewhere in the back of her mind, she swore she had seen that man before.

C. A. Simonson

CHAPTER 18 - SIMMONS' STORY

Ben found Dol later that afternoon on the corner with her arms full of packages. "Did you buy out every store?" he teased with a wink as he helped load the packages into the trunk.

Dol gave him a childish grin and got into the car.

"You'll never guess why Simmons wanted to see me," Ben blurted without waiting for her to ask.

"Don't keep me in suspense. Tell me."

"Simmons wanted to make a confession. He thought I would be the better person to talk to since I'm a lawyer. Besides, he didn't know how to contact Frank."

"But we already knew he killed Pa. He admitted that before."

"Admitted while he was drunk, remember? He claimed we coerced it out of him. That wasn't true, but he thought he had grounds to claim innocence. Today was different. Today he wanted the God-honest truth to be known."

"I remember he said he hadn't meant to shove Pa hard enough for him to fall on the tines of a broken pitchfork, but it did the job."

"Your father was drunk that day too. They were in a nasty fight that ended with that shove and fall. Your pa was already battered, bloody, and bruised when Simmons found him, according to his story. But here's the strange part: it's *what* they were arguing about that led to the fight. That's the key to this whole situation."

"They were fighting over Frank because he wouldn't go with Simmons, right?"

"Nope."

"Because Pa told the boys to work as free labor for Simmons as payment for his gambling debt?"

"Nope." His mouth turned into a grin.

"Come on, Benny," she whined and rolled her eyes as she punched him in the arm. "Tell me the reason. I'm dying to know."

He chuckled at his wife. He loved to get a rise out of her. "Okay. Okay." He patted her arm in mock attempt to calm her down. "They were fighting over Guy."

"Guy? Why?"

"Guy lived with Simmons for a while and worked on his farm to pay off your father's debt – that much we know. We also know Guy ran away from Simmons, and then came back to confront your pa and maybe even to warn your brother Frank to get far away from him."

"Yeah, all that was in Guy's letter to Frank. So?"

"Here's the clincher—" he paused dramatically and waited for her response.

"Ben-neeee...."

He inhaled deeply, let out his breath in a slow whistle, and then to build the suspense, he said in a whisper, "Guy was Simmons' child."

Dol sat back in her seat and stared at him in amazement as she took in his words. "His child? Simmons' child? How?"

"Simmons' story about your mother was partially true. He and she were together at one time, but never married – only long enough to have a child together. A boy."

"Guy?" She was skeptical.

"Yep. They named him Ervin. Simmons and your ma separated soon after the baby was born. Guy never knew Simmons was his father because your pa, LeRoy Larue, adopted and raised him. Guy went by his middle name and the last name of Larue."

"Do you think Guy knows Sy Simmons is his real father?"

"Ooooh, yes," Ben let out another low whistle. "Simmons said the truth came out when he went to get Guy the second time. Your pa put all the blame on Guy for being born, and according to Simmons, it got ugly."

"But Guy went to work for Simmons, right?" Dol tried to piece it together.

"Yes, for a while. Simmons said it lasted a few years but it wasn't a good fit. Guy was madder than a hornet at LeRoy for putting him in that situation, and of course for lying to him. Then when Guy found out your pa was apt to pawn Frank off to Simmons as gambling pay too, it made him even angrier. The final straw was when your pa said he never belonged to him in the first place – that he was Simmons' kid."

"Probably why Guy had a fight with Pa in the first place?"

"I would say it was a good reason. I'd be rather angry if I were in his shoes."

"Simmons said Guy ran away from the farm. He went to retrieve him – twice. That's when Simmons started to pursue Frank to come live with him. He thought Guy would be more cooperative if he had a brother to live with him, so he went after Frank. That's when Guy took off. Simmons said he supposed Guy went back home to warn Frank, and he followed. In any case, Guy met up with your pa first, and we know what happened then."

Dol shook her head, her face scrunched into a frown. "Poor Guy. And then he ran off thinking he'd killed Pa. Remember? His letter said that's why he joined the Navy."

Ben nodded. "Guy had plenty of reasons to take off, but not good ones. I hope and pray Guy didn't die at sea thinking he was a murderer. If he's alive, we must find him and set things straight. He has to bring closure to that part of his life."

"I agree. Guy needs to know the truth to set him free of unnecessary guilt and know that we're still family, no matter what."

They rode quietly for the last several miles, deep in thought. Finally, Ben had to ask. "Speaking of family, you still have two younger sisters somewhere. You told Frank you were going to search for them. Have you called the orphanage? After so many years, maybe they'll be more willing to give you information."

"I've tried a few times, but always get the runaround. Their policy is to not give any data on families where children have been adopted, especially to biological family members seeking information. But I promise to try again and see if I can dig up something. There have to be files on Josie and Gracie. Someone has to know something."

"Maybe there's a way I can help...." Ben thought aloud.

C. A. Simonson

CHAPTER 19 - NEW HOME–NEW HOPE

"So much has happened to you since I saw you two weeks ago – a new job and a new place to live..." Grace gazed out Jo's second-story window. "This place is just perfect for you."

"It's small, but it's much larger than what I had before," Jo's face beamed. "I'm just glad to get out of the dump I was in."

"How did you find this apartment?"

"Remember the young man I told you about? 'Mr. Tall, Dark, and Handsome?' He lives in these barracks – right around the corner, in fact. He told me about it. He and his friend are supposed to deliver a couch in a little while. I want you to meet him," Jo's eyes twinkled at her secret. She plopped down on the floor.

She went on, "It's called Huskerville. These apartments are part of the complex; it's like a city within a city. There's even a hospital here. It's for people who work on the Air Force Base, at the plant, at the hospital, and in all the little stores. Now they've opened up apartments for university students too."

"But you're not a student...."

"Not yet," Jo interrupted with a giggle. "My guy," she giggled at her inside joke, "pulled some strings so I could move in early. With my new job at Charlotte's Café, I'll get more money plus benefits. I'm so excited!"

"Jo, I am so happy for you."

"I hope to earn enough money waitressing to enroll in the college next spring. I've always wanted to be a nurse. This is my chance. The college has a great nursing program. Maybe I can get a job at the hospital eventually."

"That's wonderful!" Grace pondered the question before she asked it. "Jo...Father would help you with college expenses if you asked."

Jo's bright mood suddenly soured. She folded her arms and her face went dark. "I'll never take another dime from that man as long as I live. Never."

"Why? He has it to offer."

"Not for me."

"He would be so proud of you."

"Gracie, you don't know John like I do." She rose from the floor to redirect the conversation. "Want a soda?"

Grace nodded. As Jo headed toward the kitchenette, there was a knock on the door.

"Oh, goodie! The guys are here with my couch!" Jo forgot about the sodas and ran to let the men in.

Guy and Jack backed their way into the apartment with a small couch in tow. "Where do you want it, beautiful?" asked Jack.

Jo blushed a warm pink and pointed to the

vacant spot under the picture window.

They set the couch down, and Guy went over to give Jo a squeeze. "We found a chair to match too," grinned Guy, his eyes glued on Grace. "Jack, could you go grab it?"

Jack's face screwed into a grimace, but he nodded and went back downstairs.

"This must be your sister, Grace?" He smiled and held out his hand. "I've heard a lot about you."

Grace stared at the tall man who towered above her, slightly uncomfortable with his gaze fixed upon her. A nervous giggle escaped her lips as she took his hand to shake it. "Jo, is this your man?" she half-whispered under a cupped hand.

Jo shook her head and looked at Guy. Both she and he broke into laughter. "Grace, I have a big surprise for you. You may want to sit down," she pointed to her new couch with pride. "Do you remember anything about our big brother, Guy?"

She cocked her head and scratched it as if trying to pull out a memory. "I barely remember him. I remember Dolly more because she took care of us. Why?" Her curiosity piqued.

"You were so tiny and young when we were told to go sit on the fence and wait for Pa to come back home. Pa hung you on the fence by your coat because you were too small to balance on top. Do you remember that? Remember when we slept in the old barn full of moldy hay? I slept on one side of Dolly, and you curled up in her arms on the other side. Remember?"

She scratched her head again. "I remember some things, but not much," she admitted as her forehead creased into a wrinkle. She kept her eyes on the tall man with the black wavy hair and bulky muscles.

"That was close to fifteen years ago. Guy, our oldest brother," Jo looked up at him with admiration and a smile, "helped us as much as he could, and then he went to look for Pa."

She nodded in mild confusion, and folded her hands on her lap, not sure what all this talk had to do with anything. Guy maintained his gaze upon Grace while Jo talked. Grace shifted her position on the couch and blinked nervously.

"I only remember that Pa never came back and we ended up going to the orphanage with Dolly, and then the McMillans adopted us."

"Well, let me introduce you to our big brother, Guy." She wrapped her arm around his, "He's back from fighting in the war. We have our own war hero, Sissie."

Guy's smile exuded love for Grace. "You're a beauty, Gracie. My baby sister has grown into a woman. You look so much like Mama."

Grace blushed and lowered her chin.

"Come here, both of you," he held his arms out for an embrace. "I'm so happy to find my little sisters." Guy inhaled with deep satisfaction as he squeezed the girls. "Now, if we could only find the rest of our family."

"I've been working on that. I contacted the orphanage and asked about Dolly. Found out she moved to Fremont shortly after we were adopted. That's not far from here. Maybe she still lives there."

"Good news and good work! Maybe we could all take a run up there someday and look around."

The girls nodded their agreement.

Jack hauled the chair up the stairs and entered with a red face and feigned breathlessness. He set the chair on the floor and collapsed into it, brushing the sweat from his forehead.

"You poor boy," Jo teased. "Have a seat, won't you?" She pointed to the chair he had already sat down in. "I'll get you something to drink. Colas for all?"

Jo pretended to hand Jack the cold bottle of soda, and then pulled it away before he could grab it and gave it to her brother.

Guy grinned as he observed the playfulness between Jo and Jack. "Quit messin' with my sister, Donner."

"Me?" Jack put on a sad face. "I think it's the other way around. You have some beautiful sisters, Guy. I'll give you that. And I understand this redhead is still available." He grinned at Jo. She blushed.

Grace had not taken her eyes off her brother. "You're so handsome, Guy. Does he look anything like Pa, Jo?"

"Hmmm.... Well, don't recall Pa's features very well. Pa had red curly hair, didn't he, Guy?"

Guy nodded and blinked, old memories coming to the surface again. He bit his lip. "Think I took more after Mama's side of the family."

"I'd love to hear all about you," Grace said. "What made you go to war? What was it like? When did you get back? Do you have a girl? Are you married? I don't see a ring on your finger."

Guy laughed. "You're an inquisitive one, aren't you? Too many stories for the first day."

"He was courting a young filly in Hawaii," commented Jack. "She was a beauty." He whistled low.

"What happened?" asked Jo.

"Things didn't work out as I would have liked. Maya liked me, but not enough to come back to the States with me," Guy explained.

"Hawaii? You lived in Hawaii too?" Grace's jaw dropped in awe.

"The Navy hid us there for a while after our ship sank—to protect us from the Japanese soldiers," Jack explained.

"Your ship sank?" she asked in amazement. "How did you survive?"

"Almost didn't. In fact, I thought I had wanted to die..." Guy's voice sobered as he paused to look out the window. Past thoughts flooded his mind again," ...but that's a story for another day."

"Well, someday I want to hear them all!"

"Guy, guess what?" Jo's eyes lit up. "I got a new job! I'm now a waitress at a little café downtown."

Guy nodded his approval. "Good. More than good, it's excellent. About time you got away from Duffy's bar."

"What?" Jack uttered in feigned distress. "You mean, my cute little redhead won't be there to serve me?"

Jo reddened at the mention of Duffy's in front of Grace and attempted to change the subject. "Better news: Grace is getting married."

Grace blushed and giggled. "December 31st, and I can't wait. Just think, now I'll have both my brother and sister there."

"I wouldn't miss it for the world, Gracie."

"I think everything has started to change for the better," Jo thought aloud.

"In more ways than one," Guy agreed.

Jo frowned. "How so?"

"Well, for one, you and Grace are doing well," he grinned with a nod of approval. "My Navy buddy, Tink—rest his soul—always said, *'If you keep looking up, good things are going to happen; you only have to have faith.'* I believe that more and more every day. You've found your big brother who wants to protect you both; you've got a good lead on where to find Dolly; you now have a great job without all the riff-raff," he pointed toward Jack, who made a face at him, "and a new home with new friends." Again he pointed toward Jack. Jack nodded with a grin and a wink toward Jo.

"I would call that quite amazing grace, Jo. Wouldn't you?"

CHAPTER 20 - VISIT TO OVERBROOK

Ben snuck up behind Dol as she peeled potatoes at the kitchen sink. She jumped as he wrapped his arms around her waist and kissed her on the neck.

"Benny Ryan. You startled me. Lucky for you I didn't scream. The kids are napping."

He chuckled. "Sorry, Sweets," he folded his hands in mock repentance. He walked over to the refrigerator to forage for a snack.

"Get out of there, Benny. Supper will be ready in an hour."

"Worse than the kids – that's what you always tell me," he laughed and patted her on the bottom.

"Benny. What's gotten into you today?"

"Just playing with my beautiful wife." He leaned against the counter to watch her work. "I'm going to Lincoln again tomorrow. Want to ride along?"

Dol's face lit up. She loved to shop in Lincoln, and there were still a few gifts to buy. Her smile faded as she made a pouty face. "I would love to come with you, honey, but I can't. I have to measure a lady for a dress tomorrow, and then hem four dresses. I didn't realize how much time three children could take up when you have a home business. Wish I could come, but not tomorrow."

"Oh well, maybe next time."

"By the way, when you're there, you'll have to eat at the little cafe' downtown. Excellent peach pie à la mode – your favorite. Charlotte's Café on O Street."

"On your most worthy recommendation, Madam, I will plan to indulge myself this decadent pleasure." He bowed again.

"Oh, Benny," she laughed. You always know how to make me smile. "Are you going to see Simmons again?"

"No," He paused. "I have other business to tend to. Something's not right at Overbrook Orphanage."

"What do you mean?"

"You told me you've contacted them several times about your sisters, right?"

"Um-hmm."

"And although they know who you are, they still can't tell you anything about them– even though a number of years have passed. What did they tell you?"

"Policy."

"Wasn't there something else?"

Dol put down the knife to stare out the kitchen window; it helped her think. "Yes. Yes. There *was* something strange. The lady on the phone told me there was no record of a Josie or Josephine Larue. That can't be right. There have to be records of her. We all entered the orphanage at the same time.

Where's her records?"

"That's what I intend to find out. Someone is hiding something."

"There's the lawyer in you coming out again," she said with pride.

"That's right, and I may be able to dig deeper than you could. They may respond more quickly to a lawyer than to a sister. Say a prayer that I find what I need."

Ben pulled his car into the parking lot at Overbrook Orphanage, a formidable, large stone-and-brick, four-story building. Light snow dusted the beautifully-landscaped grounds. He walked in and introduced himself to the receptionist.

"I am here to speak with the administrator," Ben announced. "Marva Smarkel is expecting me."

The lady nodded and called the administrator's office. Soon Miss Smarkel came to the front, greeted him, and led him back to her office.

"Please, have a seat." She motioned to the chair by her desk. "What brings you here today? Do you want to adopt a child? A little girl perhaps?"

Ben cocked his head. "Oh, no. I have three children of my own. They're enough of a handful. I'm here to obtain information about some girls who lived here over a decade ago."

Marva Smarkel squinted at the man through her low-setting spectacles. "I see. And for what purpose?" She removed the pencil stuck through her upswept bun.

"I must locate two girls. A family has asked me to help find them. An urgent matter has come up."

"Well," she tapped the pencil on the desk with a stern schoolteacher look. "It's Overbrook's policy..."

Ben cut her off. "I know Overbrook's policy, Miss Smarkel," his voice as stern as her look. "As a lawyer, I also know you, as its administrator, can override that policy." He narrowed his eyes and stared back at her.

She shifted uncomfortably in her chair, shoved the pencil back into her bun, and glared at him. "Just who *are* these girls?"

"Josephine and Grace Larue. They were four and six years old when they first arrived – about fourteen or fifteen years ago."

Larue again. Third time this month. She pursed her lips and said in her tight, squeaky voice, "Wait here. I'll see what I can find."

He watched the skinny spinster click-clack through the doors on her stick legs poked into too-tiny heels. He picked up a *LIFE* magazine from the table and thumbed through it while he waited.

Half an hour later, Ben began to wonder if she would return, or if she had left the building. Dol had informed him Miss Smarkel was a difficult person to deal with; it would be even more challenging to get any information from her. He was almost ready to call it a wasted day when he heard the sound of high heels clipping on the linoleum floor.

"An emergency meeting came up," explained the receptionist, "but Miss Smarkel said I could give you copies of what you requested." She handed him a brown folder.

Ben quickly flipped through the pages. "This is Grace's information, but I see nothing on Josephine. I need her files as well."

"If she was six when she arrived, that would make her around age twenty-or-so now. Correct?" The receptionist was smug.

Ben nodded with tight lips.

"Miss Smarkel said we expunge all records after a child reaches their twentieth birthday."

Ben frowned at the news he knew to be false. "And if someone tries to locate them?"

"It is our policy...."

Ben waved her off with a shake of his head. "Thanks, anyway." He would have to be satisfied with what he got – for now.

Before his drive home, Ben decided to find the café Dol had mentioned and have lunch. Charlotte's Café was easy enough to find. He grabbed a newspaper on his way in, found a booth by the window, and opened the folder while he waited for the waitress. He leafed through the pages.

> *Grace Ellen Larue. Born August 22, 1932, Tekamah, Nebraska.*
>
> • *Abandoned child.*
> • *Biological mother: Mary Iver Larue, deceased.*
> • *Biological father: LeRoy Henry Larue, location unknown.*
> • *Adopted December 10, 1936*
> • *Adoptive parents: Mr. and Mrs. John McMillan (Joan) 3255 S. 38th Street, Lincoln, Nebraska.*

The record continued with health facts, behavior, and more, but Ben had what he needed. He now had the address for the McMillans in Lincoln. If Grace was there, no doubt Josie was too. He peered out the window. *The girls are old enough to be out of school and perhaps away at college.* He determined to locate the family anyway and ask them a few questions.

The waitress came to take his order of burger, fries, coffee, and a promise of peach pie à la mode to follow. He opened the copy of the *Lincoln Times* and flipped through the pages with disinterest. He hoped to find something worthwhile, but it appeared there wasn't much going on in Lincoln. He noticed a huge ad on one page for *McMillan Industries,* a large manufacturing plant. He wondered if John McMillan was associated with it. He flipped past the news, the comics, the sports, and had reached the announcements page when the waitress came with his food. He stopped short when he glanced at an engagement announcement in the paper.

"Pretty, isn't she?" said the waitress.

Ben studied the picture and an eerie feeling washed over him. The girl in the picture was the image of his wife when she was younger. A closer look told him the rest of the story:

Grace Ellen McMillan, daughter of John and Joan McMillan, Lincoln, Nebraska, engaged to William Lee Ericksen. A December wedding is planned.

Ben couldn't believe his good luck. *No*, he corrected himself, *it was God's good grace that led him here and Dol's prayer being answered today.*

"Miss, may I keep this newspaper?"

"Sure, it's yesterday's news anyway."

"Thanks, and what's your name?"

"I'm Jo."

"Thanks, Jo. You've been a wonderful waitress today."

Ben left her a generous tip and hurried out the door, anxious to get home and tell Dol his news about Grace.

C. A. Simonson

CHAPTER 21 - BEN'S NEWS

"Dol!" Ben bolted through the kitchen door so fast it made her jump. "You'll never guess what I found out today!" His eyes beamed with excitement.

"You got the information on the girls from the orphanage?"

"No, that's another story." He held the brown folder up for her to see."

Her eyes lit up. "Well, sit down and tell me already," she poured them both cups of coffee and motioned toward the kitchen table. She waved a fresh-baked chocolate chip cookie in front of his nose.

Ben took the cookie and stuffed it into his mouth, and then laid the newspaper in front of her. It was folded open to the announcement. "Who do you see?"

Dol glanced over the picture. "A very happy couple," she tilted her head and gave him a quizzical look. "She could almost pass for me."

He rolled his eyes. "Look closer."

Dol read the announcement aloud:

Grace Ellen McMillan engaged to William Lee Ericksen.

"Grace Ellen is my baby sister's name." Dol's eyes widened in excitement. "Benny! Do you think it could be...?" She was almost afraid to hope.

He grabbed her by the waist and spun her around with a hug. His excitement matched hers as he nodded. "We've prayed for years to find your sisters. Today God has answered our prayers!" He laid the brown folder from the orphanage on top of the paper. "Look."

She opened the folder and read:

Grace Ellen Larue, brought to Overbrook Orphanage, October 1936, by sister Dolores Louise Larue. Adopted by John and Joan McMillan, Lincoln, December 1936.

Dol continued to read the rest of the record in silence as tears of joy slipped down her cheeks. "Benny..." she choked back her tears, "you've found her. I can't believe it." She looked from the record to the newspaper and shook her head. "You've found Gracie, and she's getting married. My, my. Look how grown up she's become – my baby sister."

"I picked up the newspaper at the little café you'd told me about. The orphanage gave me her records. It gives the McMillan's address. And if Grace is there...."

"...then Josie must be too," she finished his sentence. Dol dabbed at her eyes as she flipped through the pages. Her heart was full of excitement as she searched through the information. "Wait— there's nothing on Josie, Ben. What about Josie?

There's no mention of her at all – not even of my bringing Josie with Grace to the orphanage. All three of us were processed in together."

"I know. It's very odd. The orphanage said there were no records on Josie Larue. Said she may have never been there. We both know that's false. I sense a cover-up. A search warrant will allow me to investigate the home's records further."

They were quiet for a few moments as Ben stuffed more cookies into his mouth and put plans together in his head. Dol struggled to fit all the pieces together in her mind.

"You said you went to the café," she said after a few minutes. "Did you have the peach pie I told you about?"

"Yes, I did, and it was fantastic. A little redhead waited on me. Great gal."

"I think she was the same one who waited on me. Did she have long, naturally curly red hair? Cute, with blue eyes?"

Ben nodded. "Said her name was Jo...." his voice broke in mid-sentence. The light went on in both of their heads at the same moment as their eyes widened with new realization.

A shiver went up Dol's back. "Could it really be?! Could it really be Josie? How is it possible not to recognize my own sister?" Dol put her head in her hands.

"It's been over fourteen years. Jo's grown up," Ben tried to offer explanation.

"We have to go back down there and find out if it's really her." Dol sat deep in thought. "You know, when I left the café, an older man bumped into me and nearly knocked me down. He looked familiar, but I couldn't place him. He was very gruff and unapologetic. Now I wonder if he was the man who adopted the girls – this," she pointed to his name on the adoption papers, "this John McMillan. I have vague memories of him from the day he picked the girls up at the orphanage, but my view wasn't clear from the third-floor window. Now I'm sure; it must have been him. He looked furious, and Josie didn't seem happy to see him."

"Maybe we should pay the McMillans a visit too," Ben said as he got his pen out to jot a note. "Ready for another road trip to Lincoln, Mrs. Ryan?"

CHAPTER 22 - CAFÉ REUNION

"Butterflies" was not the word Dol would have used to describe the feeling in the pit of her stomach. Flutters of excitement and anticipation, yes, but her gut was tied up in knots.

"I'm really going to see my sister! Fourteen long years – and to think she's been only an hour away all this time." Dol shook her head in surprise and frustration.

"Don't get ahead of yourself. We both hope it's Josie, but we're going on a hunch. Don't get your hopes up too high."

"Isn't that what lawyers do all the time? At least it's something to go on – more than we've had in the past. We need to find Gracie too, especially now we know she's getting married."

"All in God's time, Sweets. He'll work it out. He always does."

Jo had been down in the dumps all morning so she had invited Grace to have lunch with her at the café before her shift started. Grace would cheer her up. Jo got there early enough to hang up her coat, put her purse in her locker, and get a table in the back where they could talk, before she ordered lunch for the both of them.

How John had ever found her at Charlotte's Café was a mystery. She had taken Guy's advice and was careful to not tell anyone where she had moved or where she had gotten a job. George, her former boss, had said it was "no skin off his nose." Somehow, though, John had found her. *He has too many cronies around town to help him out of his schemes and messes. They're probably keeping an eye on me too.* Jo looked at the clock. *Almost eleven. Grace should be here soon.*

Grace entered the café looking radiant. Grace loved life, and it shone on her face. Jo loved that about her.

"Back here, Grace," she called, and waved her to the back.

"Hi, Jo," Grace waved as she bubbled with enthusiasm.

Jo smiled. "Hamburgers are on their way. Is an early lunch okay with you?"

"Does it come with lots of french fries?" she grinned as she sat down, "and a big strawberry shake?"

"Girl, you'd better watch your figure, or you won't fit into your wedding dress."

Grace gave a little pout. "Okay. Only half an order, then."

They both giggled. Jo was glad to have her sister back on speaking terms. Grace was a-buzz with wedding news.

"I've tried on oodles of wedding dresses. Couldn't decide on any of them. Mother said we can go to Omaha and look for other gowns. Would you come with us? You could help me pick out the perfect one. Oh! I can't believe I'm really getting married!"

"I'm happy for you, Sissie." Jo grinned. Grace babbled nonstop like she had when she was a little girl.

Jo was glad for the distraction and interaction. She needed some of Grace's enthusiasm to rub off on her today. As the girls engaged in wedding talk, they didn't notice the couple who entered the café and found a booth in the front.

Ben and Dol settled into their booth hoping the red-headed waitress would serve them. When another girl approached, Dol's heart sank. The waitress greeted them and set menus and water before them.

"I'm so disappointed. I thought we might see her here today."

"Maybe it's her day off. We can ask," Ben encouraged as he patted her hand. He hated to see Dol's sadness wrinkle her pretty face.

When the waitress came back to take their orders, Ben asked. "Last time I was here, there was a waitress named Jo – the one with red hair? Will she be in today?"

Dol crossed her fingers and said a quick prayer.

"Oh, yeah. Jo. Her shift begins at twelve-thirty today."

Dol glanced at her watch. It was eleven-thirty. She gave Ben a sideways 'can-we-stick-around?' look. He nodded reassuringly.

"However," the waitress went on, "she came in early to eat with her sister." The waitress pointed to the back corner of the room.

Dol's heart leapt into her throat as she gasped and stretched her neck to look toward the back. Her eyes twinkled with excitement as she grinned at Ben.

"Thank you, Miss," Ben spoke for Dol.

Dol's voice lowered to a squeaky whisper. "Benny. They're *here*. Both of them. Josie, and Gracie too." Her hands quivered as she picked up her napkin and dabbed at her eyes. She took out her compact, checked her face, and reapplied her lipstick. She rechecked her lips and smoothed her hair. "I'm as giddy as a schoolgirl!"

"Calm down, Sweets. Get yourself together. Big breaths." He patted her hand.

Dol giggled with excitement. "Sounds like you're coaching me in labor all over again."

"Well, aren't I?" he teased.

"I can't stand it. It's been so long. Will they remember me? Do I look okay? What will I say? Oh, Benny, this is so wonderful!"

Ben stroked her hand as love overflowed in his heart. "Do you want me to go over and get them? I don't think you'd make it over there." He chuckled.

"Oh, would you? You're right. I'm afraid my legs would crumple beneath me and I'd end up in a heap on the floor and make a big fool of myself."

He chuckled in amusement as he thought of the scene. "Finish your coffee. I'll see if they'll join us." Ben rose from the booth and went to the table where Jo and Grace were engrossed in chatter.

Dol lifted her cup with trembling hands but couldn't drink. She put the cup down quickly before she spilled it on herself. She strained to see Ben as he approached the girls.

"Excuse me, girls," he interrupted their conversation. "I'm Ben Ryan. My wife and I are visiting Lincoln today, and we need your help."

"Hello, Mr. Ryan," Jo said. "How can I help you?"

"You don't know me, but...."

Jo cut in. "Oh, I remember you. You asked for the newspaper last week when you were here. Business, you said?"

"That's correct. There was a special engagement photo in the paper. I took it home to show my wife. A beautiful couple, I might add," he nodded toward Grace.

Grace blushed, "Thank you, sir."

"My baby sister," Jo said with pride. "My gorgeous baby sister. Now, is there something I can help you with?"

A crazy idea popped into Ben's head. He decided to go with it. "As a matter of fact, there is. My pretty little wife is seated up front," he pointed toward Dol.

She put up her hand, waved halfway, and gave a tiny smile as she shivered with excitement. The girls squinted, but were too far back to see her face. They waved back and questioned Ben with their eyes.

"My wife would very much like to meet both of you. You see, she's a reporter and would like to do a quick interview with the both of you about Overbrook Orphanage."

They both jumped with a look of fright.

"How did you know we were from Overbrook?" Grace asked in a tiny voice.

"Nothing to be afraid of, girls. This will be quick." His smile disarmed them. He nodded and beckoned for them to come with him.

"Come on, Grace," Jo said as she rose from the table. "It's okay."

As they neared the booth where Dol waited, the look on their faces changed from doubt to disbelief, and then to joyful recognition. Tears streamed down Dol's face. Her body trembled the closer they came. Not able to hold herself back any longer, she scooted from the booth and ran to meet the girls in the middle of the café.

"Josie! Gracie!" She held her arms out toward

them. "I can't believe I've finally found you girls! Look at you – all grown up!"

Jo was the first to embrace her sister. "I've searched for you, too. I've missed you so much," she cried. "Grace, do you remember Dolly?"

Grace wept. She fell into Dol's arms and clung to her like a young child who had just found her long-lost mother. She couldn't speak; her body shook as tears flowed. "Dolly...you...you...came back...."

Patrons of the café clapped their approval and enjoyed the drama being played out before them. Embarrassed, the girls blushed, making their faces shine all the more. They were so wrapped up in emotion that they didn't see John enter the café and head straight for Jo.

C. A. Simonson

CHAPTER 23 - ROUGH ENCOUNTER

John made a beeline for Jo, determination written on his face. He marched up to the women, pushed Dol and Grace to the side, grabbed Jo's arm until it made her wince, and began to pull her aside.

"Josephine McMillan. You are coming with me!" He shouted at her.

"John, stop." Color drained from Jo's face as she stared wide-eyed and embarrassed as she caught sight of her boss on the phone with his eye on her and the disruption of the wild man.

"You owe me, Jo," he swore.

Ben and Dol stared in disbelief. Dol knew this had to be the man who almost knocked her down before in this very café – the man from the black sedan who took her sisters years before.

"Father!" Grace ran to Jo's defense. She grabbed at his arm and tried to pry it away from the gorilla-clutch he had on Jo. "What are you doing?"

John pushed Grace so hard she fell to the floor. "I'll deal with you later, Princess." He turned toward Jo. "Thought you could hide from me, did you?" He swore, his voice rising a decibel with each word as he jerked her toward the door.

"Benny, do something," Dol pleaded.

Ben was already on his feet. With clenched fists, he pushed his body between John and Jo, loosening John's grip on Jo's arm. She escaped his grasp and rushed to Grace who sat dumbfounded at the scene.

"This is none of your concern," McMillan growled. "Jo is my daughter, and she needs to come with me. Now."

Anger renewed, she rose from Grace's side. "I do *not*," Jo dared to defy him. "And I *will* not! I am not your daughter, and I won't be treated this way by you any longer!"

Oblivious to the stunned patrons watching his outrage, John raised his hand to strike her as the police came through the door.

The policeman grabbed McMillan's arm in mid-air. "You're under arrest for disturbing the peace and for creating a civil disturbance." He read him his rights and handcuffed him.

"This is insane! Jo is my daughter."

"Not the way to handle it, sir," the soft-spoken policeman replied. "You get the opportunity to think that over downtown at the precinct."

John swore. "You don't know who I am! I'll be back, Jo," he called over his shoulder on the way out the door. "You can count on that."

The sisters gaped as an irrational John McMillan was hauled off the premises.

"I'm so sorry," Jo apologized with tears in her eyes. Her happiness had suddenly turned to sadness. She helped Grace off the floor. "Grace, are you alright? I'm so sorry."

"Jo," called the manager. "Need to see you a minute." He motioned with his hand for her to come to the back.

"Please," she looked at Dol with fearful eyes. "Don't leave. I'll be right back, I promise. Please wait. I'm sorry."

Dol nodded with a sorrowful look as Jo walked to the back with her head down. *What in the world had this girl lived through?*

Grace was stunned. She took a seat beside Dol. "I don't understand. I've never seen Father act that way before."

"He's the man who adopted you and Jo?"

"Yes. That was John McMillan. He's an important businessman in Lincoln. Owns a few companies, the biggest being McMillan Industries, a manufacturing plant. He's known for getting what he wants."

"Guess his name won't do him much good now," commented Ben.

Jo came back to the table in slow, measured steps with her head hung low. She wiped at her reddened, swollen eyes. Her face was flushed.

Dol took the girl in her arms as a mother would a child, and let her sob. "I don't know what's going on, honey, but I care, and I want to hear all about it."

"Well—" Jo sucked in her tears, "if you

want...you can come...to my place. Then...we can get reacquainted..." her voice came in spurts between sobs. She tried to smile, but her eyes brimmed again.

"Don't you have to stay for work?" Grace wondered.

"No, Sissie. I...have all the time...in the world." Jo's attempt at a laugh sounded like a wounded animal. "John just got me fired."

CHAPTER 24 - MEETING THE MCMILLANS

Ben and Dol followed Jo to her apartment in Huskerville. Dol was shaken by the events.

"Jo's rattled."

"For good reason. Her adoptive father makes a scene at her workplace and ends up getting himself arrested and her fired. Some father he is," Ben pinched his lips.

"Thank you for agreeing we should stay and visit this afternoon, Ben."

"I'm an emotional mess," Jo's hands shook as she unlocked the door of her apartment. Her legs wobbled beneath her as she led them in. She threw her coat across a chair and motioned for them to do the same. She gazed at Dol through flooded eyes. "I don't know what to say...." Her tears would not remain at bay.

Dol's motherly instincts took over. She took Jo in her arms and cradled her. "Go ahead honey. Cry. Get it all out."

After a few minutes that seemed like hours, Jo pulled herself together, wiped her eyes, and dragged a stool from the kitchen. She took a huge breath and released it slowly as she perched upon it.

Grace was beside herself. "What's going on, Jo?

Why did Father act like that toward you? What did he mean, 'you owe me'?" She threw her hands in the air.

"You have to know, even though I hate to tell my story. I'll tell you what's been going on. It hasn't been pretty. In fact, my life has been pretty ugly. Grace, you've been kept in the dark way too long."

"I'll sit out here," Ben said, "so you girls can talk in private." He pulled a stool up to the kitchen counter that separated the two rooms.

Jo took Grace and Dol into her tiny living room within earshot of the kitchen. "Remember our last day all together?"

"Yes, I'll never forget it. It was Thanksgiving when all the children at the orphanage were allowed to eat together and then share the day," Dol thought back.

"I remember," added Grace. "Jo and I helped prepare name tags. I was so excited that I giggled all day and couldn't be still. We were happy to see you again, Dolly. We hated that you had to live on another floor away from us. We never saw you, except for special occasions."

"It was hard," agreed Jo. "We always looked up to you for help and advice when we didn't know what to do, and then all at once we couldn't do that anymore." Jo dabbed her eyes and blew her nose, overcome with emotion again. "I'm so glad you're back, Dolly. I've needed you so many times."

Dol put her arm around Jo again and gave her a

squeeze while she nodded her concern.

"So then Jo became my big sister, even though she was only six," said Grace. "Thinking back to that Thanksgiving Day, it was when we told you about the McMillans, wasn't it? Except we didn't know their names then. We just knew a couple had come to the orphanage a couple weeks earlier and were looking around, like they were inspectors or something."

"You didn't see them at first, Grace," Jo interjected. "But I noticed them. A tall, nice-looking man and a lady with blond hair walked our floor where the four-to-six-year-olds lived. They looked at all of us girls, and then at you and me again, like they were sizing us up. It made me curious, but afraid. I thought we were in trouble or something."

Jo sat quiet for a moment as the memories flooded back. "I remember how much the lady reminded me of Mama and I told Grace. I missed Mama so much."

"And I didn't even remember what Mama looked like anymore," confessed Grace.

"I told Grace how pretty Mama was, and how the lady had blond hair just like her. The next day, Miss Smarkel called us to her office. Said she had a surprise for us. Remember how scared we were when we sat on the couch in her office?"

"Yes, I do," Grace said as she shook her head at the memory. "It made me think of our first day at the orphanage when the preacher and his wife brought and left us there. I was so scared I squeezed Josie's hand until her fingers turned red."

"Neither of us knew why we'd been called into the administrator's office that day," said Jo. "As far as we knew, we'd done something wrong."

Dol nodded with understanding as they told their story. She had had her own frightening times seated on that same couch in the administrator's office.

Josie continued. "Miss Smarkel smiled her crooked, quirky grin. It looked suspicious. That old spinster never smiled unless she had something up her sleeve. She told us not to worry and said, 'You'll like this surprise'. Then she told us to wait, and left us sitting on the couch alone."

"That's the day it all started...."

Jo and Grace looked at each other and made scary faces as they remembered the day long ago.

"What's going on, Josie?" little Gracie's face crinkled with fear. She scooted closer to her sister.

"Dunno. But don't let go of my hand, Gracie. Understand?"

Gracie nodded fiercely as her little legs swung back and forth over the edge of the couch. Her eyes darted from the administrator's door back to her sister. She snuggled even closer.

Miss Smarkel returned in a few moments with a handsome man and a pretty, blond-haired woman. Josie recognized them immediately as the couple she had seen the day before roaming the halls.

"Josie. Gracie. Someone very special wants to meet you," squeaked Miss Smarkel.

The girls stared wide-eyed at the couple, trying to understand why these people would want to meet them. John McMillan stood tall at six-foot-two, a handsome man with dark brown hair and broad build. Dressed in a suit and tie, his businesslike appearance made him seem older than his thirty years. He put his arm around his wife, Joan, a woman in her late twenties with soft, sparkling blue eyes and long, blond hair, pulled into a stylish French twist. She knelt down in front of the little girls and took Josie's right hand and Gracie's left hand.

Gracie clutched Josie's other hand all the harder; Josie winced.

"Hello, Gracie. Hi, Josie. What pretty little girls you are. My name is Joan." She smiled at Gracie, and then let go of their hands.

Josie relaxed a little, but did not let go of Gracie's hand. She gave the lady a tiny smile and admired her gold-cross necklace. She was pretty, just like her Mama.

"And I'm John," said the tall man. He nodded to the administrator. "She's perfect, Miss Smarkel. Do you agree, Joan?" he questioned his wife.

She nodded with a hint of tears in her eyes. "Yes, John. Perfect in every way."

"Do you have any questions for the girls?" Miss Smarkel wanted to know.

"May I talk to them in private? They may not want to talk in front of us all, and I don't want to scare them," Joan spoke in hushed voice.

Miss Smarkel nodded, and she and John McMillan went into the back corner of the room, leaving Joan with the girls on the couch.

Joan McMillan sat down between the girls, forcing them to let go of each other's hands. Gracie started to reach for Josie's hand again, but Joan took it instead. "There now. I would like to know about you girls. Would that be all right?"

They nodded and shrugged their shoulders, but their faces filled with apprehension. Josie eyed the man standing off in the corner speaking to Miss Smarkel. She couldn't hear what they were saying, and it bothered her. She stuffed her hands underneath her bottom so Joan couldn't hold them.

"What are your favorite colors, Josie?"

Josie had to think a minute. She had never thought about it before. "Yellow," she finally said. "Like the sunflowers in our back field at home."

Gracie nodded her assent and smiled.

"Remember when we picked some for Mama last summer, Gracie?"

Gracie nodded. "Yes. Yellow."

"Do you like dolls or stuffed animals?"

"We've never had a doll or stuffed animals," Josie answered for them both.

"What about puppies?" Joan lowered her voice to a whisper.

Both Josie's and Gracie's eyes lit up at the question. *Why was she asking all these things?* Josie fretted.

"Can you stand up so I can see how tall you are?"

Josie was reluctant. She didn't like all these questions but she obeyed, and slid from the couch to stand. Gracie followed her lead. Joan stood as well. Josie stood a couple of inches higher than Joan's waist. Gracie was a head shorter.

"Good. Let's see," she said as she tapped her finger on her chin, "I would guess about a size seven-eight for Josie and a size four for Gracie. My, my, you're a tiny thing," she wound one of Gracie's golden curls around her finger.

Gracie looked up into the lady's sky-blue eyes. Her heart melted at the woman's touch.

"You're right," Miss Smarkel spoke up, "that's their sizes exactly. You may sit down again, girls."

"Yes, indeed. Perfect. Obedient. Quiet. Respectful. She'll be a wonderful addition to our family," John McMillan said.

"Such wonderful news!" Miss Smarkel high-pitched voice squealed as she clapped her hands. "Let's go into my office in the back and finish the paperwork."

"If you don't need me, I prefer to stay with the girls, John."

He nodded and left with Miss Smarkel.

"May I sit between you again?"

"It's okay, I guess," said Josie as she slid over to make space between them.

"I have dreamt of this day for years, girls. Now it has come true." She picked up their hands again.

"John and I have always wanted a little girl, but I couldn't have any children of my own. My heart's been empty without a child to love."

She stroked Gracie's hair. "I looked just like you when I was a little girl, Gracie. You have blue eyes and blond hair just like me."

"I hope I'm as pretty as you are someday."

Joan McMillan's melodic laugh sounded like an angel's song. She wrapped her arms around the child and squeezed tight. "You are more than pretty now, sweetheart." Gracie melted into her embrace. It had been too long since she'd felt a mother's love.

"And Josie, you're a beauty too!" She turned and attempted to hug Josie.

"I resisted her hug from the start. I sensed something was wrong," said Jo. "Grace, you were infatuated with Joan McMillan that day, as if you'd met your own angel."

"She *was* my angel – and always has been like one to me."

"She's given you everything you've ever wanted," she cleared her throat. "Another story," she crinkled her forehead at Dol.

Dol turned her head in understanding.

"It worried me when John McMillan came back into the room and announced that everything was 'all done'. He looked very satisfied with himself. Joan ran to him and threw her arms around his neck. He said he had to take care of a few more details with Miss Smarkel. They thought I couldn't hear them, but I did," Jo continued the story.

"I heard Miss Smarkel tell him the sisters couldn't be separated. He nodded and told her they'd have to get things ready on their end and would be back before Christmas to pick us up. Smarkel told them she'd have us ready to go."

"The couple said goodbye and left. Josie and I sat there and looked at each other, wondering what had just happened. Miss Smarkel suddenly turned all businesslike again, told us we did a good job and that we had made a very good impression on our new mother and father. Then she sent us back to class," said Grace. "Just like that."

"Just like that," repeated Jo.

"When we got back to our rooms, Grace squealed and twirled me around until I was dizzy. She couldn't wait to tell you all about it, Dol, but I wasn't quite sure how to feel. I was confused and scared."

"I was so excited to get a new mama and papa," said Grace.

"I remember that Thanksgiving Day well," said Dol, thinking back. "It struck fear in my heart to hear what you told me, Grace."

CHAPTER 25 - THANKSGIVING MEMORY

"Thanksgiving was only a few days away, and one of the few times we were allowed to gather for a meal together," Dol thought back.

"We hardly ever got to see you, and I missed you so much. Special occasions and holidays were the only times we saw each other," Grace agreed.

"I really tried to find a way to see you girls more often. I want you to know that. It broke my heart that I couldn't see you every day. I remember how both of you ran toward me as I came downstairs to the dining hall that day. Grace, you almost knocked me down!" Dol laughed as the memory came alive again....

Little Gracie couldn't contain her excitement. "Guess what?" She ran and threw her arms around Dolly's waist, making Dol stumble for balance. Grace giggled.

Dol hugged her little sister tight, and then sat on her haunches to look Gracie in the face.

"What, Sweet Pea? You're bubbling over!"

Gracie cupped Dolly's cheeks in her hands to focus on her sister's face. "We're getting a new mama and papa!"

Dolly almost toppled off balance at the news. She gave her friend, Jenna, a frightened look.

"What?" She raised her eyebrows. She looked at Josie with an 'is-it-true?' look, but Josie just shrugged her shoulders and looked at the floor.

"Well? Is it true, Josie? Or is Gracie just making this up?"

"I...I...think so. I'm not sure," Josie hedged.

"It's true, Dolly," Gracie defended with her little hands on her hips. "And we're all going. They said so. And they're getting us puppies and dolls and a yellow room and everything."

"Gracie, you don't know that," Josie scolded.

"Do too. She said."

"Gracie—who said so?" Dolly started to reprimand her for telling stories. "Who's 'she'?" Her voice betrayed the worry she felt. She shot Jenna another look of alarm.

"The pretty lady," Gracie defended in innocence. "The lady with blond hair. She was real pretty and smelled real good and told me I was pretty too and said that I looked just like her when she was a little girl and that I could have anything I wanted forever," she bubbled without taking a breath.

"What's her name?"

"Joan. And the real tall man's name was John and they're really nice and they look really rich and the lady had on a pretty gold necklace with a gold cross and wore a real soft furry coat."

"What exactly did they say?" Dolly directed her question toward Josie. She was getting more concerned by the minute.

"I overheard Miss Smarkel say they couldn't separate the sisters. What's that mean, Dolly?"

Gracie made her voice sound high to mimic Miss Smarkel. "She said 'Good job, girls. You made me proud. You made a very good impression on your new mother and father.'" Gracie giggled. "I'm so excited! And we get to be there for Christmas! Maybe we'll even get a puppy, Josie!"

Dol took a deep breath. "Those words you spoke that day knotted my stomach into a tight, ugly ball. Jo, you asked if the couple had talked to me too, because you assumed we would all be adopted together. But Miss Smarkel didn't tell me about anyone being interested in adopting you girls. I had hoped you had gotten your stories mixed up, or had misunderstood what was said. Grace, you were intrigued and quite enamored by the lady, and couldn't stop talking about her gold necklace and soft fur coat. But Jo, you weren't so sure about things, were you?"

"Joan had told us they couldn't have any children of their own. She said we were making her dream of having a little girl come true, but somehow I wasn't convinced. John was handsome and seemed nice. He was so tall he had to stoop to go through the doorway. At least I thought he was nice—until the day they came to get us," Jo grimaced at the remembrance.

CHAPTER 26 - TRUTH BE TOLD

"I remember the day they came to get you. Made my heart almost stop beating. I was mad and scared and confused."

"How could you remember it, Dol? You weren't there. I tried to run back inside to tell you where we were going," Jo said, "but Miss Smarkel wouldn't let me. I was frantic with worry."

"I know."

"But how?"

"I watched everything from my third-story window. I had nursery duty every afternoon. I rocked the babies by the window so I could look outside, and then put them down for naps. One day, I saw the black sedan drive up front. I was curious when I saw the fancy, rich-looking couple get out and come into the building. A while later, I saw Miss Smarkel march you girls out the door with the couple following behind. Then I watched you run back toward the building. It even looked like you called my name. It tore me up inside. It looked like you gave her quite a fight, Jo."

"I didn't want to leave without you, Dol," said Jo. "I didn't know until that minute that you weren't coming with us. When I found out, I was mad – and then afraid. I tried to come back to tell you, so you wouldn't worry about where we'd gone."

"It made me livid when that man...."

"John," interjected Jo.

"...when John picked you up and forced you into the back seat of the car. He treated you so rough. I watched you scream and cry. Broke my heart. I wanted to run out there and swoop you into my arms and rescue you. I wanted to hold you and tell you everything would be all right, but I couldn't leave the babies. I didn't know what to do. I was frantic too."

"He hurt me that day," Jo confessed, "in more ways than one. But that was just the beginning." Her face was drawn. She wrung her hands as she spoke. "He continued to hurt me until the day I ran away."

"Jo!" Grace gasped. "What do you mean – hurt you? The McMillans did nothing but good for us. They provided us everything we ever needed or wanted."

"Joan spoiled you rotten, Sissie. That's true. But I didn't have it as good as you. Joan got the daughter she always wanted – you, Sissie. John got me."

Confusion showed on Grace's face. She ran her fingers through her hair, and then scratched her head. "What are you saying, Jo?" Grace didn't like the thoughts that entered her mind.

"I never liked that man from the beginning.

From the first day he told Miss Smarkel we were smart, quiet, and obedient, and then when he shoved me into the back seat of the car the day we left, I suspected something was wrong. That day, he whispered words in my ear that made my bones go cold."

"I saw him do that," remembered Dol. "What did he say to you?"

"He said if I didn't do everything he wanted, he would hurt Grace. I believed him. Dolly," Jo teared up again, "I *believed* him."

"It's okay," Dol said. "You're away from him now. Tell us about it. We're your sisters. We're family. We're here for you."

"I've always hated that man." She grabbed a hanky to dab her nose.

"Jo, I know you've never liked Father, but why?"

"He made me do terrible things. Things I hate to talk about. Every time he wanted something from me, he'd remind me of his threat to hurt you. I was afraid he'd do something bad to you. Did he ever hurt you, Sissie?"

"No. Father's always been good to me."

"Has he ever asked you for special favors?"

Grace thought a moment, and then shook her head. "Whenever I wanted anything, I asked Mother. She would persuade Father. I never had to go to him for anything."

"Joan was never fond of me."

Grace screwed her eyelids into her forehead. "Jo, what do you mean? Mother has always loved you. And so has Father."

"Too much, Grace. John loved me too much. That's what I tried to warn you about before I left and we got into that big word fight."

"Oh. That. When I wouldn't listen to you," Grace nodded with new understanding.

Jo nodded. She got up and got sodas out of the refrigerator. "Remember how they gave us our own bedrooms when we became teenagers?"

Grace nodded. "Mother wanted us to have our own special places – rooms we could call our own."

"Yes, but that's not the only reason, Sissie." Jo's eyes went dark. She closed them tight as she recalled her personal horrors. She finger-combed her thick, red curls and pulled them into a ponytail as she contemplated how to phrase her thoughts.

"Did he ever hurt you, Sissie? Did he ever ask you for favors in return for something...?"

"Never."

"Tell me the truth." Jo stared her in the eye. "Did John ever touch you, well, you know...." She couldn't bring herself to say it.

A look of horror washed over Grace's face. She put her hand to her mouth. "Are you asking...?"

Jo nodded, her face grave.

"Jo!" Grace's voice was stern. She folded her arms to resist the awful words she heard. "I am ashamed of you! No! Father would never do anything like that!"

Jo simply nodded with uplifted eyebrows. "He did – to me."

Grace curled her legs underneath her and wrapped her shaking arms around them. She shook her head in disbelief. She didn't want to hear these cruel words. All she had thought to be true began to crumble beneath her.

Jo continued in a small, defeated voice. "I could count on him like clockwork whenever he got good and drunk – like Pa. He would always say I 'owed him.' Never understood what that meant. That's when I ran away the first time. After graduation, he moved me into an apartment downtown. It was okay for a while...." Jo's voice faded.

"Is that when I thought you had left for college?"

Jo nodded.

"Still can't believe they lied to me about that."

"The apartment would have been grand if everything had been on the up-and-up. But John began to visit me more often, if you know what I mean. I got fed up, so one day I threw the key at him and found my own place to live. I was afraid to call you, Gracie, and so ashamed. I wanted to warn you, but couldn't. And then he found me again. It seems no matter where I go, he finds me and it starts all over again. I hate this life." Jo bawled. "I feel like such a bad person. How could you even look at me now that you know what a bad person I am?"

Dol had put her hand to her heart and rocked back and forth as Jo told her story. She felt torn all over again and hated to see the sadness on Jo's face. She rose from her seat, went over and wrapped her arms around Jo once more. "I wish I could have been there for you, honey."

Jo sobbed. "I wish you could've been there, too, Dolly. I'm such a bad person. How could you still love me now that you know what I am?"

"Jo— It's not your fault. And there's nothing you'd ever do or go through would change my love for you. You're my sister," said Dol. "We—" she motioned for Grace to join in the hug, "are your sisters and we love you unconditionally."

"I didn't know," Grace said, dismay and shock still on her face as she rose from her chair and entered into the warm sister-embrace. "But, Dol is right. We're family. I'll always be here for you too."

"Grace, you have to move out of that house, far away from John."

"I'll be married in a couple of months, and then I'll be gone. But if what you said is really true, I'm not so sure I want Father to walk me down the aisle."

"It's true, Grace. Sad, but true. Ask him yourself."

"I think I will. I'll see what he has to say for himself."

Dol saw Ben point to his watch – his unspoken signal for time to go – and nod. She nodded back.

"I hate to break up this grand reunion, ladies, but Dol and I really must head back to Arlington." Ben gathered their coats.

"I really don't want to leave when I've just found you two," Dol said as she rose to her feet, "but we do need to get back home." She gave them each another long hug. "It's only an hour away, but our Lizzie will be home from school soon, and we still have to pick up Molly and Timmie from the sitter's."

"We finally found each other and there's so much news to catch up."

"You're right!" Dol's eyes brightened with a new thought as she put on her coat. "Listen. Thanksgiving is coming up in a couple of weeks. Why don't you girls join us for dinner? We'll have all day to visit and catch up. Besides, I want you to meet my children. How about it?"

"That would be swell!" Grace responded for the both of them.

"Guess I don't have to work," Jo said with a sarcastic smile. "Yes. It will be good to have better things to talk about."

"Good." Dol gave a joyful clap as she grinned at Ben. "I'll plan a very special Thanksgiving family meal we won't forget. And Grace, bring your fiancé if you want."

Ben and Dol left with mixed emotions. Dol was overjoyed to have found both sisters, but her spirit churned in turmoil at Jo's rugged past.

Something nagged at the back of Ben's mind on the way home. "Do you suppose Jo's awful circumstances could have anything to do with the orphanage not having her records?"

"That's an interesting thought, Benny."

"I plan to check into it."

They fell into deep thought on the ride home. Ben wrestled in his mind how he would get to Overbrook's records, while Dol planned a scrumptious meal in her head for a special time with her sisters.

The girls plopped on the couch after Dol and Ben left, weary from the strenuous day. They felt a new release and joy with the discovery of their oldest sister.

Suddenly, Grace jumped up and went to look out the window. "Jo! We forgot to tell her about Guy!"

CHAPTER 27 - CONFRONTATION

"Mr. McMillan," your daughter, Grace, is here to see you."

"Send her in." He had wondered if Grace would come see him, or if she would send her mother to talk to him about the incident at the café. He hadn't been able to settle things yet with Jo since the incident occurred. He didn't want to explain his actions to Joan or to Grace. It was none of their business as far as he was concerned. He had paid the fine at the police station for disturbing the peace and thought that was the end of it. As Grace entered, he peered around her to see if Joan had come too.

"Well, hello Grace," his tone was cordial but not welcoming. "What brings you here today? Is your mother coming?"

Grace did not return his greeting or the smile. She coldly stood at his desk and stared at him.

"You usually go through your mother whenever something's on your mind."

She looked over his desk of papers and noticed the large picture of Jo, but none of herself, nor of her mother. She gave him a scowl.

"Sit down and talk to me."

"I will stand, thank you," her icy words matched

her cold blue, accusing eyes. "Father, what got into you yesterday? It was like you became another person I've never known. You pushed me down, and then you attacked Jo and told her she 'owes you'?"

McMillan maintained his composure and leaned back in his black leather swivel chair and studied Grace's face. He took several seconds before he responded. *She has become quite bright in spite of Joan's awkward attempts to keep her sheltered.* "I'm not sure what you're talking about, Princess."

"You know good and well what I'm talking about, Father. The café yesterday? The encounter with Jo that got her dismissed from her job? Has your memory dulled so soon?" Grace fired the words like darts at his heart.

"Watch your tone, Princess." His eyes narrowed. "It was just a little misunderstanding between her and me, that's all. We'll get it straightened out."

Grace mirrored his look with disbelief. "I can't believe you're lying straight to my face!" With determination, she planted herself in the chair in front of his desk, and folded her arms. She stared at him with disgust. "Don't lie to me. What have you done to Jo? I demand to know what's going on."

She felt a shiver as his face grew cold.

"Careful, Grace. You're treading on dangerous ground. You dare not demand *anything* from me.

You don't know what I can do."

Grace dared to press harder, although her insides quivered like jelly. "What have you done to her to make her leave home? Why did you drive Jo away?" Grace spoke through clenched teeth as her fury grew. She wanted to hear the words from his own mouth.

"Jo left on her own accord." His tone announced a finality. His eyes gave warning to ask no more.

Grace knew she shouldn't press it, but she had to know. She reared to her feet in anger. "I don't believe you. Not anymore. I don't know *what* to believe anymore." She stuffed her hands into her pockets so he couldn't see them tremble. "But I think I'm starting to believe Jo."

John's face hardened and his eyes narrowed. "What has she told you?" He leaned forward and popped his knuckles.

Grace's muscles tensed as she heard the sound. "I won't repeat such horrible acts. But—" she was afraid to look into his eyes, "she's told me enough." She forced herself to look at him. "Is it true? Is what Jo told me really true?"

The veins on John's neck enlarged as blood rushed to his head. She swallowed hard.

"Jo is a habitual liar, a rebel. Always has been!"

Grace's eyes shot darts at his heart. "That's a lie! Jo is a kind, giving, and loving sister."

"Grace." John's voice felt like gravel on her

skin. "If you believe anything Jo's told you, and insist on siding with her, you may as well move in with her. You'll have no place in my home."

Grace glared at him. "Are you threatening me? You'd actually kick me out?"

John surprised her by a sudden wicked laugh. "You are either a very brave girl to bring accusations against me, or stupid like your mother." He held his cynical stare. "She is not worth your time, Grace. You are much more beautiful than that whore ever was. If I were you, I would rethink your decision on whom to believe and whom to call a liar."

Grace was appalled. Her eyes got larger with each discriminating, vicious word as she stared in horror at the arrogant man who stared at her with contempt. "Jo is my sister, and I will *never* disown her. She's my real family."

"Then you cannot be a part of *my* family. Sorry, Princess," he sneered. "And if you keep going down this road, you'll force me to pull the purse strings on your wedding account as well. Think it over."

Grace's mouth dropped open. She quickly put her hand over it to stifle the words that threatened to spill out. She stumbled backwards a few steps. In all her eighteen years, she had never seen this side of John McMillan.

"Mother would never hear of it," she dared to whisper.

"Your mother has nothing to say about it – or

about anything else I do, for that matter."

"Fine. So be it. And you can forget about walking me down the aisle, too. I'll not have any part with you."

As she spun around to march out the door, she heard the low mutter, "So be it, Princess."

C. A. Simonson

CHAPTER 28 - REPERCUSSIONS

"Grace. Grace. What have you done?" Joan McMillan pulled at her hair, beside herself. "You should never have gone alone to see your father." She put her head in her hands. "You don't know him like I do."

Grace busied herself packing clothes in boxes and cleaning out her closet. "I think I'm beginning to understand him a lot more, Mother. I saw a whole new side of him today."

"I've tried to shelter you from that side of him, but I know a whole lot more than he gives me credit for."

"So you knew Jo really wasn't at Princeton?"

Joan hung her head. "Your father thought it was best for you to not know where your sister went. I really didn't know where she was, but I did know she wasn't at college. I...I just wanted to protect you."

"Protect me from whom? Jo? From her influence? From her boyfriends? Who, Mother?"

Joan shrugged her shoulders; she reached for her necklace and began to rub the gold cross.

"Did you know she was in Lincoln this whole past year?" Grace's voice rose.

"Your father rented an apartment for her

downtown for a while, but then she left. I don't know where she went. Thought maybe she ran off to live with her friends again."

"Do you know why she left?" Grace's temper boiled.

"She wasn't happy. Jo was never happy here. She didn't appreciate anything we did for her. She only wanted her way, and to get away."

"But, Mother, do you know why?"

Joan bit her lip and grasped her necklace. "She didn't love us. Even after your father gave her everything...."

Grace cut her off. "You're wrong. Father abused her. From the day we came into your home until she left," she clipped her words in anger, "...and he still is."

"Grace! Shame on you for saying such things! Who told you that?"

"Jo."

"It can't be true!" Joan's eyes widened in fear and disbelief.

"Tell me you didn't know."

Joan's forehead wrinkled in confusion and doubt as the revelation took root in her head. "Maybe..." she stammered for words. "Maybe Jo exaggerated. Maybe she mistook your father's affection for...ah, for...something else?"

"No, Mother. Jo lived the horror. Father told me if I take Jo's side, I'm not welcome here, so if that's how it's going to be, I'm leaving." Grace tossed the items from her dresser drawer into a box.

"Please, Grace. You can't leave me here alone. What will I do? Where will you go?" Joan followed her down the stairs to her car.

"I'll figure it out. William and I will be married soon, and then we'll have a place of our own. I was oblivious, and concerned only for myself. That's my excuse, Mother. What's yours?"

Grace gave her mother one final look as she walked out the door. Joan crumpled by the front door. Her hand clutched at her heart as she began to sob. "Gracie— it was never supposed to be like this."

"George!" John raged down the stairs from Duffy's brothel rooms above the bar. "Where's Jo? I demand to see her! Now!" He slammed his fist on the bar and searched wildly around the room. "Where is she?"

George rushed from the kitchen when he heard the racket. "McMillan, I don't care how important you think you are in this city, you will not demand anything in my establishment. Now lower your voice and calm down, or get out."

John put both hands on the bar and leaned in to face George. "Jo's room is empty. Cleaned out. Where is she? Where'd she go?"

"Moved out."

"What? When?"

"Couple of weeks ago."

"Where?" his voice raised. He grabbed George by the collar. "Where'd she go?"

Unmoved, George calmly but firmly removed John's hand and frowned. "Don't know. Don't care."

John's temper erupted. He swiped his hand across the bar crashing bottles and glasses to the floor.

"McMillan, you're drunk. Leave. Now – before I call the police. And don't come back."

"I'll find her, you know," he muttered as he stormed out the door.

Grace drove off in a huff in her little Mercury Coupe, leaving Joan McMillan in tears at the door. Grace drove a few miles to the edge of town and pulled off to the side of the road. She put her head in her hands, lay across the steering wheel and wept. Her emotions were mixed and her brain was a jumbled mess.

She was shaken – first by her father's unexpected behavior and the turn of events, and then by her mother's weakness in dealing with it. She hadn't counted on consequences being doled out when she lashed out at her father. She hadn't expected him to react as he did, and although she didn't really think he'd carry out his threats, she couldn't be sure.

I hope it doesn't affect William's job offer at McMillan Industries. What will I tell him? Will he understand? Maybe I pushed Mother too far. What will Father do to her? She worried.

She could move the few boxes and clothes into the house William was fixing up for them, but it was too early to move in. *What will I do? Where will I go?*

Grace dared to pray for the first time in her life. *Help, God. I need to know what to do....*

A quiet stillness permeated the car. Grace calmed as she stared out the window at the snowflakes beginning to fall. Then an idea came to her. *Jo will know what to do.* A new determination enveloped Grace as she turned the car west and headed toward Huskerville.

CHAPTER 29 - THANKSGIVING SURPRISE

"Hi, Dolly," Grace greeted her sister on the phone. "Do you mind if we bring a guy with us for Thanksgiving dinner?"

"Of course, Grace. That'll be fine. I'm excited to meet him." Dol gave Grace directions to their country home outside Arlington, and then hung up.

"Another person coming?" asked Ben.

"I think she plans to bring William, her fiancé."

"All set, Jo," Grace giggled. "Dol has no clue, even though I said we were bringing a guy. Get it? Guy?" She laughed again at her own joke. "She thinks I'm bringing Will."

Jo giggled too. "It will be the perfect surprise. I can't wait."

Guy picked up the girls early Thanksgiving morning so they could spend most of the day with Dol and Ben. They chatted and their excitement mounted as they neared Fremont, and then headed toward Arlington. As they pulled into the long drive of the Ryans' country home, Grace and Jo could barely contain themselves.

"You go in first, girls," Guy said. "I'll hang back a bit."

"They're here, Mama," Lizzie called as she peered through the front window. She opened the door before they could knock. "Come in," Lizzie invited.

Dol rushed to the door, her eyes fixed on her daughter with a slight frown. "Lizzie," she scolded the seven-year-old in a half-whisper, "what have I told you about opening the door to people you don't know?"

"But, Mama, you said *you* know them," Lizzie pouted, feeling the reprimand. Dol smiled in spite of herself.

"It's okay, Sweetie – this time." Dol patted Lizzie on the back. "Go get Molly and your Daddy. Tell them our company's here."

Jo entered first and Dol pulled her in close for a hug.

"My sweet Jo! So good to see you again. How are you doing after that awful experience last week? I felt so bad for you. Believe me, my Ben intends to look into your...." She saw Lizzie and Molly enter the room. "...your...ah... shall we say...problem."

"Oh, Dolly, no. I don't want to be a bother. Really. It isn't necessary. Best to leave it alone."

Dol held her at arm's length and looked her square in the eye. "Listen to me, Jo. It *is* necessary. We're a family, and now that we've found each other, we must support each other. That man is stalking and abusing you and Ben intends to prove it. He's an excellent lawyer, and he's good at what he does; let him do it."

Jo nodded, reassured. She stepped aside to let Grace greet Dol.

Grace wrapped her arms around her oldest sister's neck. "I'm so glad to have you back in our lives, Dolly."

"Grace, my sweet little Gracie. What a beautiful woman you've become!" Dol hugged her tight. When she looked over Grace's shoulder, she saw a man standing by the doorway. Their eyes met and Dol's heart skipped a beat. He looked oddly familiar. He nodded and waited to be introduced while Dol talked with the girls.

Guy stood back with admiration of Dolly's motherly touch with her younger sisters. She had always been the mother hen – especially after their mother died. She had nurtured and taught them, held them close, and was their guardian and protector. She loved her sisters more than life itself. To see them adopted and taken away must have been sheer torture. She probably thought she would never see them again. *Just like me.*

"And who might this be? Your fiancé, Grace?" Dol approached the man with her hand extended. He stood almost as tall as the door frame. She studied his face. Rugged and tall, his stature spoke of a man of great experience. His black eyes twinkled and a cocky grin crossed his lips as she neared him. Dol felt a shiver run up her spine. *Just how my big brother smiled when he was about to tease the daylights out of me.* She withdrew her hand and covered her mouth to stifle an excited scream. Her eyes brimmed as keen recognition dawned. She stood transfixed, her eyes locked on the man towering over her.

"What's wrong, Mama?" three-year-old Molly tugged at Dol's skirt.

Dol dabbed her eyes with her apron and looked down at her child. "Nothing, Baby. Nothing's wrong. Mama's just happy." She smiled and patted the child as tears spilled down her cheeks.

Dol reached up and put her hands gently on Guy's cheeks, shaking her head in disbelief and wonder. "He once was lost, but now is found. I've found my big brother. Hello, Guy. I've missed you." She threw her arms around his waist and buried her head into his chest as happy tears washed her face anew. "I won't ever let you leave again!"

"Hi, Sis," Guy choked as he held her tight. "It's been way too long."

CHAPTER 30 - SMALL TALK

Dol's mind spilled over with questions, going one hundred miles a minute in every direction. "How is this possible? Where did you find him? Did you girls know where Guy was all along? Do you know how long we've been searching for him? We've got to call Frank. Come. Sit down. We've got to talk. Dinner is almost ready."

Dol led them into the living room and sat down, and then stood up again. "Oh, my. What am I thinking?" she giggled, almost in hysterics. "Guess I'm not thinking, I'm too excited! This is unbelievable! What a wonderful surprise! Girls," she called for her two daughters.

Lizzie and Molly ran to their mother's side. Molly hid behind her mother's apron while Lizzie grabbed her mother's hand, still unsure if she had violated a rule by opening the door to these people.

"Stand pretty and smile." She stood them side by side. "This is Lizzie, my seven-year-old." Lizzie did a little curtsy. "And this is Molly. She's three. Girls, meet your Uncle Guy, Aunt Grace, and Aunt Jo." Molly bowed, unable to match her sister's actions. "You can go play until dinner's ready."

The girls ran to play in the other room as Ben

entered carrying their toddler. "This is Timothy Benjamin. Frank helped deliver him eighteen months ago when he came to visit." Ben lowered the wiggly toddler onto the floor, and reached to shake Guy's hand. "And this is my amazing husband, Ben. Benny, my big brother, Guy. He's *here*! I still can't believe my eyes." She hugged him again and dabbed another stray tear from her eye.

Ben pumped Guy's hand and grinned from ear to ear. "You don't know how happy you've made your sister. You've been in our prayers a long time."

Guy returned the hearty handshake with a quizzical look.

They all settled in the living room to chat while the turkey finished roasting in the oven. Guy inhaled deeply. "Smells delicious, Dolly. I've been looking forward to this – in more ways than one," he chuckled.

"You've given me the best surprise of my life. I'm so thankful you're alive, and thank God you've been found. Frank has been combing through books and calling all the naval stations in the country in an effort to locate you. You were a hard one to find. Did you girls know where he was all along?" she asked her sisters.

"We found him only a few weeks ago. In fact," Jo said, "he was the one who found me when I worked at Duffy's Bar & Grille." Jo went on to tell about their encounter. "My mouth dropped open too, when I realized it was Guy."

Grace giggled. "Jo thought she'd met the man of her dreams in this tall, good-looking sailor from the war."

Jo blushed. "Sissy...."

"Well, you did. You told me how he was a good prospect...."

"Okay. Okay, but that was before I knew it was Guy."

Guy sat back in the overstuffed chair, amused at his sisters' banter. He enjoyed family talk. "It was a miracle how I found Jo, really. Almost like Someone orchestrated it. I must admit, I wasn't looking for any of you. Assumed everyone had gone their own ways. Thought I would never see any of you again. That was a sad, awful fact, and I hated it. But, the Navy had become my family. If truth were known, I used my first name when I joined so that none of you could find me."

"That explains the name 'Ervin Larue' then?" Ben said. "Frank found the name, figured it had to be you. Made him dig further."

Guy gave Ben another strange look. "You knew about the name?"

"Frank has become quite the sleuth. Can't wait to call and tell him he doesn't have to search any longer!"

"All the guys called him Erv when he came to the bar, that's one reason I didn't recognize him. Why *did* you change your name, Guy?"

"When I signed up, they wanted a legal name –

your birth name. Ervin is my legal first name. Guy is my middle name. Maybe you didn't know that." Guy's conscience tugged at him. *Partly true. They did want a legal name, but that wasn't the only reason I insisted on being known as Ervin. I have to tell them, but is now the right time?* "Then Frank must have gotten my letter?"

"The one you sent from California, yes. You mailed it to the Johnsons in hopes they would get it to Frank. Frank had left Tekamah by that time and no one knew where he was." Dol saw their questioning looks but continued. "The Johnsons saved the letter, unopened, and Frank got it when he was here over a year ago. He shared it with me. You didn't know where you were going but you hoped you would never return."

Dol looked him square in the eyes. "Frank traced you from Virginia as far as California, and then was afraid you had been assigned to the U.S.S. *Yorktown*.

"I was."

"But— that ship sank. How did you survive?"

Guy felt the rebuke and hung his head. "Then you know what the rest of the letter said, I presume." His voice was barely above a whisper.

Ben and Dol both nodded. Jo and Grace looked at each other with puzzled looks and shrugged their shoulders.

"Please tell us what you're talking about. We don't know anything about Frank," Jo said. "He went to live with Farmer Wheeler, didn't he? And then he left Tekamah? What about Jesse and Mike? Are they still with the Johnsons?"

Ben gave Dol the 'not-now' look and she responded with a half-nod. She understood.

"Oh my, so much to catch up on," she tried to keep her tone light. *No talk of murders and deaths in front of the children. This talk will have to wait until later.* "We'll talk after dinner – when the children are down for naptime. It's a long story." She took in a big breath and breathed it out slowly. She focused again on Guy. "We're just glad you came back, Guy. We need you in our family. We need our big brother, right, girls?"

"He has definitely proven that to me already," exclaimed Jo. "He was a huge help in getting me out of Duffy's and finding an apartment at Huskerville. He's also been my guardian angel concerning John. Guy has made sure John hasn't followed me as much."

"You mean stalked you," corrected Ben. "With everything you have on him, you can put him away for a long time," said Ben.

Dol returned the 'not-now' look with a frown.

"I don't know...." Jo hedged.

"Tell them your best news, Jo," Grace beamed, easing the tension.

"Oh, yeah," Jo smiled. "Another thanks to big brother Guy," she patted him on the arm, "the best news is that I may get a job at the hospital on base – like an aide to a nurse or something."

"Which will give her experience for nurse's training later on when she is accepted into the Nebraska State University Nursing Program," added Grace. The pride was evident in her voice.

"Jo! I'm so proud of you. All this in just a couple of weeks? You are a go-getter! Things are sure to turn around for you yet," said Dol.

"Everything happens for a reason. That's what my friend Tink always told me. It's because of him that I'm alive today and have reason to live," commented Guy.

"We certainly do have a lot more to talk about," said Dol. "But I just heard the oven timer sound. That means the turkey is ready and it's time to eat. Would you girls help me get the food on the table? Ben can get better acquainted with Guy. You *will* share some of your Navy stories with us over supper, right, Guy?"

He nodded with a smile. Dolly, only two years younger than himself, had also overcome a lot of adversity. He was proud of her and glad for the man she had found in Ben. He was glad to have him for a brother-in-law, and to know he had found his family again — but would they accept and love him as a brother if they knew his secret? That he had killed Pa?

CHAPTER 31 - DINNER CHATTER

"What a spread you put on, Dolly. This is delicious," Guy muttered as he stuffed another bite of turkey into his mouth. "The only thing missing is a plate of Spam." He gave her his cocky grin.

It made her smile. "Spam?"

"It was our main meat on the ship, special-made for the military. Canned meat – spiced ham. We all grew to love it. Heard it's now becoming quite popular in the States."

"Doesn't sound like something I'd serve my guests," Dol scowled.

"I'm only kidding." He laughed. "What you have here is the best, Sis. It's for sure better than when we were kids and you had to scrounge to find enough food to make a rabbit stew. You did a good job of keeping us fed though, after Ma died."

"I remember your rabbit stew, Dolly. That was the last meal we had at the shack before we left," Jo said.

"There were seven hungry mouths to feed. Had to stretch food any way I could. Thanks to Guy and Frank, we had meat. I could always count on them to shoot a rabbit for supper." She smiled at the thought. "Been a long time since I cooked a rabbit," she raised her eyebrows Ben's way. He shook his head and gave her a 'don't- you-dare' look. "We couldn't count on Pa to bring home any food, especially when he started to drink and squander his whole paycheck on booze. We were lucky to have any food in the house."

The mention of Pa made Guy choke. He excused himself and covered it over by taking a large gulp of milk.

"Yeah, Pa was a drinker, alright," Guy paused as he wondered how much to divulge, "and a gambler, I found out."

He noticed little Lizzie and Molly listening wide-eyed to every word he said, and decided to take the conversation another direction.

"Hey, what about Frank? You mentioned he left Farmer Wheeler's in Tekamah?"

"It was amazing how we ran into each other," Dol said. "Quite a miracle, in fact." She went on to explain their unique encounter over hemming a pair of trousers for Frank, and how he was there to help deliver baby Timothy. "If he hadn't been there, I could have died in childbirth."

"Like Mama did," whispered Jo.

Dol nodded.

"What about my twin, Jesse?" asked Jo. "He went to the Johnsons with Mike, right?"

"That's where I took them. The Johnsons were glad to take them in," said Guy.

"Did Frank get to be with Jesse and Mike

much?"

"The farmer put Frank in school, and he found the boys there," Dol said.

"Are Jesse and Mike still in Tekamah?" Jo was hopeful. "I would love to see my twin brother again."

Dol shook her head with a somber look. "We'll have to continue that story after dinner," she tilted her head toward her daughters, "when the children are down for naps."

They nodded, eager to know, but curious about why the conversation would be something the children shouldn't hear.

Guy tried to lighten the mood, although he was still in the dark as well about his brothers. "Girls, let me tell you a story about Dolly you may not know," Guy grinned and winked at her.

Dol gave him a questioning frown. "Be careful now, Brother," she grinned.

"Your sister," he nodded at Jo and Grace, "your mama," he grinned at Lizzie and Molly, "once ate worms."

"Ewww," Lizzie said. "Mama, you really ate worms? Squishy, slimy ones?"

Dol howled with laughter. "Oh, Guy, that was a terrible trick you played on me. It was when I was your age, Molly," she focused on her little girl and held up one finger. "Only one worm, but it was a humongous earthworm. Your Uncle Guy told me the big bull that lived between the outhouse and the shack would chase me if I didn't eat the worm. The bull was fenced in, but I didn't know he couldn't get out."

"I dangled that fat old worm in front of her nose," Guy demonstrated to the children, "and let it stretch way out to make it look even longer." His laugh was infectious. "I wouldn't let your mama pass until she ate the whole thing."

Lizzie and Molly made awful faces at each other as they imagined the taste of an ugly earthworm. Lizzie pretended to choke.

"Uncle Guy promised if I ate the worm, it would be my insurance the bull wouldn't chase me. He told me my worm-breath would be my protection, and the bull would leave me alone." Dol shook her head at the memory. "See what you missed, Grace and Jo? Guy never teased you babies like that. I made sure of it."

"That's just plain horrible!" Jo said with a grin.

Ben was amused. "Sounds like something I would have done."

"Benny! Thought you were on my side," Dol pursed her lips into a pout and gave him a playful punch.

They all laughed. Guy enjoyed the banter. It was good to be with family again. Real family. Having his other three brothers here would have made it complete.

"Okay, Guy. Your turn – if you want to play this game." Dol scratched her head as she tried to pull a memory from the past that would out-do his tale.

"Oh, we played lots of games, didn't we, Sis? Had to think up great ones while we sat on that old fence out back – something to keep our minds busy."

"... and that's another story. You played lots of dirty tricks on the boys and me, but one time it backfired," she smirked. "I'm thinking about the 'Milk Duds story'...." she paused with flair to get his reaction.

He groaned at the memory and shook his head. "That's a far reach back – when I was too young to know better."

Jo and Grace leaned forward in anticipation. "Tell us already."

Dol knew she had their attention when they laid their forks down. "Sometimes, and it was rare, Pa brought home a box of candy for us kids to share. There were only four of us kids then: Guy, me, Frankie and Mikie."

"You were about six or seven, Guy?" Ben asked.

"That's right. Pa brought home a five-cent box of Milk Duds for us all to share – quite an extravagance for him. If I remember right, he gave me two or three pieces, and then handed the box to Dolly. He told her to share the candy with her younger brother, Frankie. Mikie was still in diapers."

"So I took the box," Dol agreed, "gave Frankie one or two pieces because he was only three, and I ate the rest."

"You always *were* Pa's favorite," Guy teased.

"I was the only girl," defended Dol with a whine. "But Guy," she rolled her eyes at him and grinned, "had an unusual feast later that night when the rest of us had gone to bed, didn't you, Guy?"

"An awful surprise was more like it. Since I was the oldest, I had to help clean up before I could go to bed. Mama and Pa were in the other room. When I swept the kitchen, I spotted three Milk Duds on the floor. I was so excited. Figured Dolly or Frank had dropped them, but I found them. Finders, keepers, you know." Guy cringed.

"And without even thinking, he popped all three pieces in his mouth at once," Dol howled. Ben and the girls had puzzled looks.

"Why is it so funny?" asked Grace.

"They weren't Milk Duds at all, Grace. They were droppings from Mikie's diaper." She couldn't stop laughing.

"And I was the lucky guy who found them. Still makes me gag." Guy pretended to stick his finger down his throat.

Everyone laughed at Guy's antics.

Dol rose from her seat at the table and began to gather plates. "Now, who's ready for dessert?"

CHAPTER 32 - FOR LOVE OF BROTHER

Ben put the children down for naps as Dol gathered the family in the living room for dessert and coffee. She finished the story of how Frank found her because he needed a pair of trousers hemmed for Mr. Wheeler's funeral, and then how he had been there for her in the traumatic delivery of baby Timothy. She caught them up on the sad deaths of their other two brothers, Jesse and Mike, at much too-young ages.

The girls wept as they heard the stories. "Frank was there for them at the end," she consoled. "He had a tough time in reconciling his feelings toward the Johnsons for a long time, but he finally made it right with his soul."

Ben entered the room and the mood lightened. "The children are down, but not happily. They wanted to be with their new-found aunts and uncle. I had to convince Lizzie to stay quiet in her room for a while."

Dol nodded. "She thinks she's too old for naps. Guy, I still can't believe you're here. It's so good to finally have you home."

"Tell us. What made you decide on the Navy over other branches of the military?" asked Ben.

"You know, when I joined the Navy, I didn't

think I'd ever see family again. The men aboard the ship became my brothers. It was great to finally have a toothbrush I didn't have to share," he grinned.

The smile on Guy's face faded. "But the reason I chose the Navy was to escape, and the ocean seemed to be the farthest away. Had to get my miserable life as far away as possible from everyone I cared about and loved...." his voice lowered to a soft whisper.

"But why, Guy?" Jo's forehead wrinkled with concern.

"If I tell you girls, I'm afraid you won't want me for your big brother. I can't risk losing you all again."

"Guy, you've forgotten, we read your letter to Frank. The one where you told him why you left to go to war," said Dol.

Guy hung his head, afraid to look at Dol or Ben.

"It's because I did a terrible thing." He put his head in his hands. His shoulders slumped with a huge sigh.

The two younger sisters frowned with questions and heartfelt concern. "It's okay, Guy. No matter what you did," said Grace. "War does terrible things to people. It changes you."

"It wasn't the war's fault, Grace. It was mine. My anger and my rage. My lack of self-control, and then my inability to cope with what I had done. All of it was my fault."

"What could be so terrible that you would want to run away and hope to die?" Jo questioned, although she could imagine a few things that terrible to want to die.

They were quiet as they waited for Guy to speak. Overcome with emotion, Guy's body shook. He looked up meekly at each one, searching their eyes for understanding, for some sign of hope.

Each one nodded their reassurance.

He took a huge breath, and closed his eyes tight. His voice was almost inaudible. "I killed Pa."

The stone-cold silence that pervaded the room chilled their bones. Jo and Grace stared in surprise and disbelief at his blunt statement. Their mouths hung open, as if waiting for some explanation.

"No, Guy...." Jo began when she saw her sister hold up her hand, motioning her to be quiet. Dol exchanged knowing glances with Ben, and waited for Guy to continue.

"Pa was cruel; he left us hungry and alone so many times. He abandoned us to fend for ourselves. He deserved what he got, but that doesn't excuse me for what I did to him. I had hoped I would die at war for my horrific deed, but when that time came and it looked like I really was going to drown at sea, it scared the liver out of me." Guy stared at the floor.

Ben, Dol, Grace, and Jo sat on the edges of their seats, waiting for his next words.

"Tell us how you survived," encouraged Dol.

"I felt so unworthy to live. I was thousands of miles from anyone out on the ocean. Alone on an empty ship – except for my friend, Tink. Everyone had abandoned ship. Tink lay wounded and unconscious from pain. I bandaged him up, and then sat beside him to guard him from the rats still running aboard. The *Yorktown* floated all night without direction. Everything was as black as night: no lights, no power, nothing. I sat there and bawled my eyeballs out. Couldn't sleep, couldn't eat. Didn't deserve to still be alive. Felt abandoned all over again."

"Guy, there's something you must know...." Ben started to interrupt.

Dol nudged him and put her finger to her mouth. "Let him finish," she mouthed.

"As I sat beside Tink to guard him from the rats that night, I recalled some of my conversations with him. Tink was very open with his faith and belief in God. He told me to have faith, even when things looked impossible. Many times it seemed as though an Unseen Presence were with us. Bullets pierced everything around us, fires burned next to loaded B26 bomber jets, plane fragments exploded on deck – and yet we were unscathed. Seemed like we walked right through some awful stuff that should've killed us time and time again. I felt invincible when I was next to Tink. Don't know if it was amazing courage, divine intervention, or unbelievable luck that kept us alive. The ship had been hit three times, and still she refused to go down. Some called it the "Miracle at Midway." She knew she still had two souls on board and refused to give up the ghost."

Guy paused to take a breath as he peered into the compassionate eyes of his sisters and brother-in-law. He saw acceptance, unconditional love, and encouragement to continue.

"Not the ship, dear brother," Dol whispered. "*God* knew there were two souls on board, and I believe God heard our prayers to bring you home safe and sound."

Guy nodded, and an uninvited tear slipped down his cheek.

"I remembered Tink's words in those dark hours," Guy said. "He told me how to find peace in my heart from all I'd run away from. He showed me how to find forgiveness from what I'd done and from who I'd become."

"And did you?" Dol laid a gentle hand on his arm, her voice only above a whisper.

Guy nodded. "The next morning, I noticed a patrol ship in the distance. Something told me to fire the machine gun. The urge was so great, I ran to find the gun and fired it into the air. The sailors aboard the other ship heard it, and soon Tink and I were rescued, and on our way to Hawaii."

"Your friend, Tink, sounds like a good man," commented Grace, wiping the tears from her own eyes. "He must have been glad to get off a sinking ship."

"Indeed he was, and he told me with his last breath to keep on believing. That's what really tested my new-found faith. Tink – my friend and mentor – died on board the U.S.S. *Hughes* moments before we docked in Hawaii. I believed his faith would save him. I believed he would live to tell the tale of survival before I did, but moving him cost him his life. His body had been critically wounded." Guy wiped his eyes with the back of his sleeve and released a huge breath.

"I'm thankful God allowed me to live to find my sisters. I'm glad to be with family again – you don't know how glad. Truth is, I found out I'm not even your real brother," Guy let his tears flow.

Grace and Jo shook their heads in disbelief. "What are you trying to say?"

"Pa told me I wasn't his son, said my real father was a man named Sy Simmons. It led to an ugly fight, and I hit him. I was *so* angry," confessed Guy. "Didn't know whether to believe him or not. That's another reason I ran away and tried to disappear. Don't deserve to be part of this family after what I've done."

"It seems we've all been through some horrendous experiences. But now that we've found each other, we need to stick together. That's what families do. I don't care what Pa or Simmons told you," assured Dol. "As far as I'm concerned, you have always been my brother and that's never going to change. Right, girls?"

The sisters nodded their agreement, although they didn't understand.

"And we already know what the fight was over. Simmons told me everything," added Ben.

Guy twisted his head as he questioned Ben. "But Pa died because I killed him. I'm sorry. I need you to say you forgive me."

"We'll do better than that," Dol said as she rose from her chair, went over to Guy, and put her arms around his neck. "Guy, you're our brother, and we're there for you no matter what, and of course we would forgive you if you needed it. The good news is: you're not guilty. You're innocent."

He lifted her arms from his neck, held her hands, and stood to his feet. "What do you mean? I saw him lying there in his own blood. It was everywhere. I hit him over and over. I saw him go down. I was out of control. He had to have died." Guy kept shaking his head, unconvinced.

"You didn't kill Pa. Simmons did."

Guy sank back in the chair as a queer look of amazement crossed his face. "What do you mean?"

"You bruised him up with a good beating," Ben said. "You gave him enough good whacks to make him bleed and pass out, but you didn't hit him hard enough to kill him. Simmons finished the job when he came to look for you at the barn that day. They fought over you. As you know, when your pa was drunk, he swung at anything and anybody.

Simmons was a mite stronger, so when he pushed LeRoy backwards, he landed on the tines of the broken pitchfork."

"The handle broke off when Pa was swinging it at me, trying to kill me. I grabbed it, and threw it down."

"Your pa's death was accidental, but it still put Simmons away in prison for a very long time. He was the one who killed him."

Guy sat back in shock as he registered the news. He let out another big breath. "And you know this for sure?"

"Heard it firsthand from Simmons' own mouth. Confessed to both Frank and me."

"I'm really innocent?" Guy sighed again and shook his head. "And all this time...." he pondered. His shoulders relaxed as a new calm came over him. So much weight had been lifted from his life.

"There's plenty of time to catch you girls up on all these stories," Dol smiled at her bewildered sisters. "But now, we need to make this reunion complete," Dol said as she picked up the phone to dial Frank.

CHAPTER 33 - A DATE WITH MISS SMARKEL

"Got the search warrants. I'm ready now, Dol. Want to ride along and visit with your sisters?"

"Wouldn't miss it. We've already planned to shop for bridesmaid dresses. Besides, that way I get to hear your news firsthand. Can't wait to hear what you find out. Do you think Miss Smarkel will allow you to look through the orphanage records?"

"She won't have a choice, Sweets. I have the official papers. Guy will accompany me for moral support, and for good measure I've asked a policeman to come along, too."

"Sounds like you have it covered." She patted him on the back.

Ben dropped Dol off at Jo's; Guy was waiting for him there. They picked up Officer Flanigan at the precinct and headed toward Overbrook Orphanage. They had agreed Officer Flanigan would present the search warrant to the administrator and stay with her while Guy and Ben searched the records for Jo's adoption paperwork. They entered the building unannounced and asked to see Miss Smarkel.

"Good morning, gentlemen," Marva Smarkel came from her office and eyed Ben with curious recognition. "Can I help you?"

"These men are here to research the home's records, Ma'am." Officer Flanigan presented her with the search warrant.

A look of fear crossed her face. "Which ones?"

"We need past adoption records in particular, and then the records of children who left the Home of their own accord." Her guarded stance made him suspicious. "Are there other records we should inspect?"

She squinted through her spectacles. "We are required to keep records for seven years – in some cases, for ten," she hedged.

"That's for financial records, Miss Smarkel. You know that. The children's personal and adoption records need to be kept forever in case any family searches for them."

"It is Overbrook's policy...." she began, but Guy stepped up to her.

"Listen, lady. Have someone show us the record room. Now!"

Miss Smarkel cringed at Guy's six-foot-two frame standing above her; she shuddered at his rough tone. With feigned determination, she folded her arms and nodded to the girl at the front desk to guide the men to the back, and remain with them while they searched. Marva Smarkel began to follow when the officer touched her arm.

"You will remain here in the foyer with me. You may as well sit down; this may take a while."

"I prefer to stand," she kept her professional

tone, but her eyes betrayed her anxiety as they darted toward the back.

Ben looked at Guy. "I don't get it. Why would she be so reluctant to let us look through the records?"

He found the box on the shelf marked 'L1935-1940' and pulled it down.

"Exactly what I was thinking, unless they're trying to keep something secret."

Ben didn't have to go through the folders far before he came to Larue. *Dolores Louise Larue* was on top. He flipped through a few folders, and then saw *Grace Ellen Larue's* folder with all its original documents. Ben noted he had received carbon copies of Grace's records. *Josephine Lynn Larue* should have been next, but there were no more Larues in the box.

"Jo's records are gone," Ben said.

"Are you sure? Maybe they got stuck behind one of the other folders."

Ben checked again and shook his head. "It looks like Miss Smarkel has some explaining to do."

He shoved the box back onto the shelf, and marched back to the foyer where a nervous administrator paced in front of the window. Ben noticed the lady fanning herself, although it the middle of November. Her worried eyes caught his.

"Did you find what you were looking for?" the officer asked.

"No. We didn't," Ben's eyes drilled a hole in the administrator. "We need the records of Josephine Lynn Larue."

"They weren't back there?" she squeaked in mock surprise. Her hands quivered as she pulled out her handkerchief and wiped her forehead. "They were there the last time I looked."

"The last time you looked," Ben drilled harder, "you told me they had been expunged – obliterated – erased. Isn't that what you said? Both you and I know that's not true. Now, you act like you don't know?"

"Listen, lady," Guy stepped up to her face again, "these are my sister's records we're trying to find. I want to know what you did with them. What are you hiding?"

Miss Smarkel suddenly felt small and vulnerable. She wiped the sweat from her forehead and eyed the policeman, then Guy, and then Ben. She covered her face with her handkerchief and collapsed into a chair by the window. Her body shook as the hardened layers of professionalism and secrecy were peeled away. Her shoulders heaved as she began to sob.

"Should we go to your office, Miss Smarkel, where it's a bit more private?"

She nodded, and Officer Flanigan helped her to her feet. She grabbed his arm for support and led the men back to her office. Guy closed the door. She motioned them toward the couch as she sank wearily into the chair behind her desk.

"Miss Smarkel," Ben pronounced his words slow and clear, "do you know where Josephine's records are? If they're not here, then where are they?"

"I was afraid this day would come," her tiny voice squeaked. She pushed at her graying hair piled atop her head in a now-disheveled bun. She hung her head. "They...are... in a safe place."

"Where, Miss Smarkel?" Ben pressed.

She put her hand to her temple and frowned, as if trying to locate the place in her brain. "Not here."

"Where, lady?" Guy demanded as he jerked to his feet and straightened his frame.

The administrator jumped in fright. "Ah...ah...." she stammered, "not here. I...I...gave them to the adoptive parents."

"You gave them the original documents and not carbon copies?"

She nodded and stared at the desk, head down. Her face looked drawn and pale as she removed her thick spectacles.

"Why?" Ben questioned. "Why would they want the original documents?"

She wrapped her arms around herself. "To erase Josephine from the system," she whispered in defeat.

"So no one could find her?" Guy's eyes grew large with fury. He thought of the pain Jo had gone through and the fearful life she lived.

"He...he promised to support the orphanage with huge donations on top of the adoption fees if I complied." Miss Smarkel bit her quivering lip. "I am so ashamed. It was wrong then, and it's wrong now. I...I know that, but the orphanage was desperate for funds. He promised to keep the money coming only if I kept quiet about it." She sighed heavily. So...I...I did."

"To be clear, you accepted hush money in exchange for expunging Josephine's records, is that right?"

She nodded again with a huge sigh and broke into tears once again.

"You really did try to make her disappear."

"By taking hush money," Guy spat in disgust.

"And he continued to support the home annually to ensure your silence?"

The truth was out. Miss Smarkel wiped her eyes, put her wire-rimmed glasses back on her nose, and glared at her accusers. "Yes. Every year. Like clockwork." *There's no use denying any more.* "The sad part is, they didn't even want Josephine. The McMillans wanted one daughter, and Grace fit the bill. I forced them to take Josephine too in order to keep the sisters together. I thought it would be better for both of the girls."

"So he made you pay for it – literally. That's extortion," Ben snorted.

She saw the officer stand and reach for the handcuffs. "Am I in trouble?" she asked, "Mister,

mister...what was your name?"

"Ryan. Benjamin Ryan, Attorney at Law. And yes, you are in more trouble than you care to know."

Ben saw the light go on in Miss Smarkel's head. "Are...are you related to Dolores Ryan, our seamstress?"

"Dolores is my wife."

"And *my* sister," emphasized Guy.

The look of surprise registered on Marva Smarkel's face as she began to connect the dots of the sordid mess she had made.

C. A. Simonson

CHAPTER 34 - DILEMMA

Dol had chattered nonstop all the way to Lincoln. She was excited to be with Jo and Grace again. The plan was to shop for bridesmaid dresses and pick up a few more Christmas gifts. Ben dropped her off at Jo's, where the girls were more than ready to be on their way. They piled into Grace's Mercury to head downtown Lincoln from Huskerville, which sat on the northwest side. Dol got into the front seat, Jo in back, while Grace drove.

"Jo, tell me about John. Has he bothered you since that time in the cafe?"

"He found out I live in Huskerville." She shrunk in her seat as she gazed out the car window.

"It was my fault," Grace admitted. "I moved out of the McMillan mansion after I confronted Father about Jo. He was furious that I would question him. I saw a side of John McMillan I didn't know existed. Mother had warned me he could get ugly, but it was more than that. He accused Jo of terrible things, and then called her a rebel, a liar, and manipulator. I said some things I shouldn't have. He threatened to cut me off if I sided with Jo. I didn't care; he made me angry with his lies."

"But she moved in with me anyway."

"Told him I would cut myself off from the McMillans before I disowned my sister. Also told him I didn't want him to walk me down the aisle because he was the real liar and manipulator. He threatened to cut off my wedding money, but I doubt if he'll follow through with it. Mother wouldn't allow it."

Jo bit her tongue. "You don't know him like I do, Sissie. Mother Joan may not have as much influence with him as you might think."

"I hope you're wrong, Jo. Anyway, it was my fault that he found Jo's place. He followed me there one day. He was livid."

"I got a restraining order on him like Guy suggested. So far, it's helped. He hasn't been around. Think I'm ready to call the cops if he shows up."

"Good for you, Jo," said Dol.

"I have to stop at the bank before we go to the bridal shop, okay? Need to get some money out of my wedding account."

"John has her set up with a limitless account." Jo rolled her eyes at Dol.

Grace wrinkled her nose. "I know. I'm spoiled." She hopped out of the car. "I'll be right back."

"All she ever had to do was ask Joan for more money, and it would be there," Jo explained.

"Lucky girl," Dol arched her eyebrows. "That was fast. Here she comes now."

Grace's face contorted as she fought to keep the

tears at bay. She bit her lip as she got in the car, and her chin quivered. Slamming the car door, she smacked the steering wheel. "It can't be. It just can't be! I'm so mad I could scream!" She threw her hands up in the air.

"Grace! What's wrong?"

"My account's been frozen. The bank says it needs John McMillan's signature before they can release any funds. Not even Mother's will do. Ugh! He warned me this would happen. I didn't want to believe he could be that mean." She put her face into her scarf and let out a low scream.

"So. Now what?" Jo leaned forward from her seat in the back.

The realization hit Grace in the face. Her source of income had died. She looked up at them wide-eyed. "You're right, Jo. Now what? What *will* I do? How can I even have a wedding now?"

"Grace, Why do you think you can't have your wedding?"

"Everything's ruined." She threw herself over the steering wheel with her face into her hands and began to sob.

"Grace— you're over-reacting."

Through muffled tones, she sobbed through her scarf. "No...no, I'm not. I haven't even gotten my gown yet. Mother and I were going to go to Omaha to shop in that fancy store there, but we hadn't set a date yet. Now, without any funds, I can't get a wedding dress, or bridesmaid dresses, jewelry, flowers, shoes...." She sucked in her breath as it struck her anew. "I can't get anything," she wailed. "I don't have a church lined up, or a preacher....and no one to walk me down the aisle!"

Dol had been quiet through Grace's outburst, unrattled by the melodrama. She reached over and stroked her hair.

"Gracie, Sweetie," Dol soothed in a calm voice. "Look at me." She cupped Grace's chin and turned her face towards her own. Grace looked up with tear-streaked cheeks. "You have a groom – William – the love of your life; you have your family who loves and supports you. All is not lost. God works in mysterious ways. He always works things out when things seem impossible. You only have to trust in His goodness."

"But what...what... about... my dress?" she wailed.

"I can make your wedding gown exactly the way you want it. I can even make the bridesmaid dresses, since it's for Jo and me."

"You...you'd do that? For me?"

"With joy, honey. We're family." She massaged Grace's back. It soothed Grace's qualms and she began to settle back.

"And I'll bet Guy would be pleased as punch to walk you down the aisle, Sissie." Jo patted her shoulder.

"Mother had planned to check out St. John's Cathedral..."

"You mean, the large church downtown?" Jo withdrew her hand in surprise.

"Yeah. But don't know if she contacted them yet."

"Don't worry, Grace. It'll all work out, you'll see. We'll help as much as we can, too. Ben and I attend a little church in Arlington. Maybe that's all you'll need. When you come up, we'll check it out."

Dol's calming voice comforted Grace. Her sister's confidence was empowering. Grace sucked in her tears and her breathing slowed. She checked her image in the rearview mirror and moaned.

"Grace, you're a mess," she spoke to her image in the mirror.

"Here, Sissie." Jo dug a half-used tissue from her purse and handed it to the front. "Grace Ellen, you *are* a mess."

Grace accepted the tissue with a quirky smile, wiped her eyes, and then blew her nose. "Oh yeah. I need a preacher to perform the ceremony, too. Do we have one of those?"

Dol laughed. "As a matter of fact, we do. Frank recently became a preacher. He can marry you. We can involve the whole family if that's what you'd like to do."

Grace's reddened face brightened with the thought. "You're right, Dol. I don't need to rely on any old bank account or on John McMillan. Maybe it *will* all work out."

"Tell you what, girls. Let's go shopping

anyway."

Grace stared. "Like this?"

They laughed. "Sure. Take us to the fanciest bridal shops you can find. We'll look at gowns and dresses, and you can tell me what you like. Then I'll have a good idea on how to make them. Sound good to you? Now wipe your face, and show me the town."

CHAPTER 35 - THE SEARCH

"Nothing at the orphanage. Where to from here?" asked the policeman.

"The McMillan residence."

The trio headed toward the extravagant Brownbilt District on the south end of Lincoln. Many new homes had been financed by President Roosevelt's New Deal and his newly created Federal Housing Administration; the McMillan's estate was no exception. The three-thousand-foot home sprawled across a few acres with beautiful landscaping with a winding road which led to the pillared entrance. The men scanned the expanse. Guy let out a low whistle. They rang the doorbell.

Joan McMillan, not expecting company, peered with caution through the peephole. Still in her robe and slippers, she felt no reason to live with Grace gone. She had been depressed and despondent since the day her daughter left her crying on the portico. Curious as to why three men would come to her home in the middle of the day, Joan checked her pale face in the hall mirror, pushed a few stray hairs behind her ear, and then opened the door. She nodded a hello to each one, and then asked what they wanted.

"We have a warrant to search your home, Mrs.

McMillan," said the police officer as he led the men inside.

A look of alarm crossed her face as she backed out of the doorway. "Whatever for?" Her voice raised in pitch as she reached for the cross on her necklace.

"We have reason to believe the original adoption records of Josephine Larue are located here in this home. If you know where they are, you'd be wise to give them to us now."

"Well, of course." She tightened her robe around her. "We have both of the girls' adoption papers. I'll go get them from John's desk."

She hurried from the room into the other part of the house with a nervous mumble, leaving a slipper behind. In a few moments, Joan came back and shot worried looks toward the police officer standing at her door. She handed the folder to Ben.

"Mrs. McMillan, these are the adoption papers and copies of official records for Grace. Where are Josephine's?" Ben asked as he rifled through them.

"They aren't there?" A puzzled look crossed her face. She ran her fingers through her hair, and then rubbed her eyes.

"We'll have to look through the desk ourselves. Please show us where it is, ma'am."

"I don't know if I should. John wouldn't approve if I...."

"He has no choice, and neither do you. The search warrant speaks for itself."

"Oh, dear," she mumbled. "If they're not here, then they must be at John's office. Why would he take them there? Oh, dear. What has John done now?" She wrung her hands.

"We believe he's hidden the records, Mrs. McMillan, and not for good reasons."

"What's this really about?" her voice quavered and her face flushed; she began to fan herself as the heat rose within.

"We believe your husband may be molesting your adopted daughter, Josie, and hiding evidence. I intend to prove he's done this heinous deed for years. And, that he's hidden her records so none of her biological family could ever find her."

Ben's blunt words caught the woman off-guard. Joan McMillan's mouth dropped open. With a loud gasp, she grabbed her head with both hands and fainted in a heap to the floor.

Guy called the ambulance, the paramedics arrived, and soon Joan McMillan was on her way to St. Elizabeth's Hospital.

The next stop would be John McMillan's office suite atop the ten-story skyscraper on the Burr Block of O Street, the center of downtown Lincoln. The men pulled up to the stone structure, its mass expanse intimidating as it loomed into the sky. Many of the major businessmen housed their companies within the skyscraper, McMillan Industries being the largest.

Ben, Guy, and Officer Flanigan stopped at the reception area in the lobby and asked to see John McMillan, president of McMillan Industries.

"Is he expecting you?" she clipped without looking at them. Her tone was crisp and formal.

"No. He is not," Ben assumed his lawyer tone. "However, he *will* want to see us when he knows what we have to tell him. It's a matter of dire importance."

"Regarding?" she stuck her nose in the air.

"Regarding Overbrook Orphanage and missing records."

The receptionist sniffed and nodded, and then called up to McMillan's office. "He said he'll see you. His office is at the top." She pointed toward the elevator and went back to her work without a glance.

The men took the elevator to the tenth floor. John McMillan met them at the door and led them to his office suite.

"What's this about Overbrook Orphanage?" he asked, his curiosity piqued.

"Right to the point. I like that in a businessman, and you look like a shrewd one," Ben said. "My name is Benjamin Ryan, Attorney at Law. This is Officer Jim Flanigan." Ben nodded to the officer to hand McMillan the search warrant.

"These gentlemen are here to search the

premises, Mr. McMillan. Here are the official papers."

"What could you possibly want here?" John's voice was cold as he folded his arms and leaned on his desk.

"I will come right to the point as well. We are looking for the official documents of Josephine Larue."

"Larue?" McMillan tried to act as if the name didn't register. "Wait a minute. Haven't we met somewhere before?" He studied the large man standing before him.

Guy smirked. "Yeah, we've met. Remember Duffy's Bar? The day you tried to work over my *sister*?" he emphasized the last word.

McMillan sneered at him. "Humph. Maybe I do, and maybe I don't. And who are you again?" He turned toward Ben. "Wait. I know you too. You were in Charlotte's Cafe the day I came to see Jo. What interest could you have in Josephine's records?"

"More like the day you came to rough her up and try to drag her away, you mean. As I said, I am Benjamin Ryan, Attorney at Law. We are here to get Jo's adoption records. We asked about them at the orphanage and they swore they didn't have them, so we made a thorough search. They told the truth; they did not have the records. Then we made a search of your home...."

"My home?" McMillan's voice rose a notch in

anger. "How dare you! What right do you have...."

"Every right, Mr. McMillan. Your wife assumed the records were in your desk; they were not. We searched your home while your wife went into hysterics. She didn't take it so well when we told her why we wanted the records, and why you may be hiding them. In fact, before she passed out, she indicated she knew something had been wrong for a long time, and figured the records must be here at your office. Now, why would you want Jo's original adoption records?"

McMillan tightened his lips in angry defiance and stared at him with contempt.

"And why would you hide them, unless you were doing something wrong and you didn't want anyone to find Jo?" Ben drilled.

No emotion nor concern for his wife. The man cares only about himself. "By the way, your wife is fine. I believe she is in good care at St. Elizabeth's." Ben shook his head.

McMillan gritted his teeth. "Fine. Help yourself," he scoffed. "Search all you want. You won't find a thing. In fact, I'll help you." He began to open the drawers of his desk and pull out papers.

"No," stated Officer Flanigan. "You will sit there in your chair while these men proceed with their search. In fact, I'll help you sit down, if you want me to."

McMillan yanked the chair from behind his desk and slammed it on the floor. He sat down and crossed his legs and folded his arms. "You won't find anything, I tell you." He put his nose in the air with a look of disdain on his face.

Ben searched through the desk drawers while Guy checked the file cabinets. They went through the books on the bookshelf. Nothing. Ben kept his eye on McMillan. *What a piece of work. No emotion at all when he learned his wife had an emotional breakdown.*

McMillan fidgeted in his chair like a sinner who had been caught in the act. Crossed, and then uncrossed his legs, drummed the desk with his fingers, wiped his forehead, but most noticeable of all, Ben noticed his eyes kept darting toward the large photo on his desk – a photo of Jo.

Ben took a seat by the desk close to the photo while Guy continued to search through books.

"Ha," mocked McMillan. "Give up already? Told you that you wouldn't find anything." His gaze veered toward the picture.

"Only taking a breather, Mr. McMillan," Ben stated in a calm manner in control of his plan. "Nice picture of Jo. Graduation?" He picked up the gold-framed portrait and pretended to admire it. "Strange that you have a picture of Jo on your desk, and none of your wife anywhere in your office – nor of your other daughter, Grace."

The picture felt a bit heavier than it should and was a bit too thick to hold one photo. Out of the corner of his eye, he noticed McMillan begin to perspire. Ben turned the frame over in his hands, and observed the man's agitation. McMillan's breaths began to come in frantic huffs. In slow motion, Ben slid the picture from its frame. McMillan's eyes grew fearful as he realized Ben had found his loot.

"Hmmmm. What have we here?" Ben feigned surprise. He pulled out a brown envelope hidden between the photo and the back of the frame. The name on the envelope was *Josephine Lynn Larue.*

CHAPTER 36 - THE ARREST

McMillan bolted from the chair with the revelation of the brown envelope. The officer laid a heavy hand on McMillan's shoulder and forced him back into sitting position.

"So you found Jo's records. It proves nothing," he sniffed in arrogance.

"Or it proves everything, McMillan," declared Ben with triumph. "You have the original records from the orphanage. We already know you paid Overbrook an exorbitant fee in exchange for these records."

"I was more than generous," he boasted with self-importance. "Everyone knows it's best to have a McMillan on your side."

Ben and Guy exchanged doubtful glances.

"Besides, we took both girls. Joan wanted a daughter. I took her to Overbrook to find one. We had planned on adopting only one child, not two, but the orphanage required that the two girls stay together. Joan pleaded with me; said she was going insane for want of a child. She persuaded me by saying we would each have a daughter to spoil. She would have Grace, and I would have Jo." McMillan played with the button on his shirt cuff as he spoke.

"But you did more than spoil her, didn't you?"

Guy closed in so that he was face-to-face with John.

"What do you mean?" He scratched his chin to put his hand between his face and Guy's.

"You wanted your way with her and no one would be the wiser. Isn't that so?"

McMillan glared at Guy in silence and chewed his lip.

"There is only one reason, as I see it, that you would want to keep Jo's adoption secret and her records hidden, McMillan," Ben hammered. "You paid the orphanage hush money. You wanted Jo to disappear from the system so no one could ever find her – as if she never existed." He poked his finger into McMillan's chest.

McMillan began to rise in protest, but the officer pushed him back in his chair. He brooded and played with his gold-engraved cufflinks as he struggled for an answer that would dismiss this whole incident.

"You wanted her for yourself, didn't you?" Guy drilled, back in his face again.

"Who told you that?"

"Jo. You mistreated her. You abused her, and you molested her. Isn't that right?"

McMillan erupted in an evil laugh. "And you're going to believe that liar? She's just a filthy slut who will manipulate anybody or anything to get her way."

Guy's fury raged as the veins popped in his neck. He grabbed McMillan by the collar, pulled him off his chair, and struck the man in the face with a hard blow. McMillan fell to the floor.

"I could grind you to a bloody pulp, McMillan," Guy swore through clenched teeth.

Officer Flanigan jumped on Guy to pull him off John before he could strike again. "Careful, Guy. I have no desire to arrest two men today." He sat McMillan back in the chair with a warning finger to stay there.

Ben stepped up to Guy and put his hand on Guy's arm to calm him. He kept his composure although he seethed within, and focused his eyes on McMillan. "You committed extortion and bought silence from the orphanage. The administrator told us you have provided them every year with a very generous, as you put it, donation since the girls were adopted. There was only one condition: that they kept Jo's adoption hush-hush."

McMillan began to laugh – a derisive laughter that mocked Ben. "You think you're something, don't you 'Lawyer Ryan'? Hah! I am not on trial here."

"You mistreated Jo from the time you got her until now, isn't that true?"

"I refuse to say another word."

"You don't have to. Your lack of words don't excuse you; they accuse you all the more. We have enough evidence to go to trial."

"We also have Jo's testimony, and you know

that," gloated Guy.

"She wouldn't dare...."

"Is that a threat, McMillan? I'd watch my words, if I were you," Ben was smug.

A twitch appeared on McMillan's face as the muscles in his neck contorted. He white-knuckled the chair, as a look of dread entered his eyes. "Tell me what you want? How much?"

Officer Flanigan lifted the man from his seat, grabbed his arms behind him, and slapped the handcuffs on him. "John McMillan, you are under arrest for alleged extortion, molestation of a child, and now for attempted bribery. There's probably much more if we look into your company's financial records."

"You don't know who I am, and you can't prove it. You don't know what I can do. Wait until you hear from my lawyer."

"And you don't know what *I* can do," smirked Ben with a wry smile. "Jo is ready to press charges and throw the book at you. She now has two sisters and a brother to stand behind her and support her, and a very good lawyer to represent her."

McMillan pursed his lips as if to swear, but instead gritted his teeth and stared at the floor in sullen and painful resignation. His wretched game was over.

CHAPTER 37 - TREACHEROUS TRIP NORTH

The sky was gray and overcast when Jo and Grace started north to Dol's. A light dusting of powdery snow tickled the windshield as the girls chatted about their day ahead. They were excited to spend more time with their sister and make plans for the coming wedding.

"Did you bring your coat, Sissie?" Jo scolded, seeing her sister in a short-sleeved blouse.

"It was so warm when we left, Jo. Didn't need it." She flipped her blond hair back from her neck. "Why would I need a coat?"

"Because it's December in Nebraska, silly. Weather can change in an instant, and the snow's starting to fall."

Grace giggled like the little bratty sister who had gotten away with something.

"You're a worrywart, Jo. Don't worry," she giggled again, "it's in the backseat. I threw it in at the last minute in case it's colder up north."

Jo shook her head and made a funny face at Grace. "You're still a brat, Sissie."

"Think we'll make it by nine o'clock?" Grace asked. "Dol wanted us there early so we could spend the whole day to measure and fit dresses for the wedding and still get back before nightfall."

"We left before eight, and it's only an hour's drive. We should make it there in plenty of time – if these roads don't get too icy and the windshield wipers work like they should."

"Wow! Look how big the snowflakes are!"

"It seems to be falling harder, too," Jo sounded worried. "We're coming to the curvy parts of the road." Jo slowed her speed in the little '48 Mercury Coupe.

Fluffy flakes soon evolved into a sideways blast, quickly piling drifts across Nebraska's two-lane Route 77. Traffic slowed to a crawl. They inched along and occasionally passed another car. They had just rounded a curve when Grace cried out.

"Jo! Watch out!" She screamed and pointed to a vehicle sliding out of control on the opposite side of the road.

As the other driver tried to compensate for the slide, he propelled the car directly toward the Mercury. Jo slammed on the brakes. The Mercury began to slide toward the ditch. Jo white-knuckled the steering wheel in an attempt to control the slide.

Grace screamed again as both cars clipped front bumpers. The other car sailed past them and landed in the ditch on the other side. The Mercury went into a spin.

"Oh! God!" Jo cried out. She took her hands off the wheel and her foot off the pedal as the car spun circles in the road. With a mother's instinct, her arm flew across Grace in protective mode. "Hold on, Sissie," she yelled. But before Jo could catch her, Grace's head collided with the windshield. She was out cold.

"Benny, I'm worried about the girls," Dol phoned her husband at work. "They were supposed to be here an hour ago."

"Were they still going to come in this snowstorm?"

"They called early and said they'd be here around nine o'clock. Said the weather was calm and warm down there then. This snowstorm sprung up out of nowhere. I'm afraid it caught them somewhere in between here and there. Sure wish there was a way to contact them."

"You know your sisters. They're probably talking and taking it slow. Maybe they got a late start."

"It's been snowing hard all morning."

"Don't worry. I'm sure they're fine, Sweets."

"Well, say a prayer, would you? I want them to get here safe."

"Will do. Let me know when they arrive."

When the car finally slowed to a stop, Jo couldn't see anything in the near-whiteout conditions. The blinding snow had turned into a blizzard. Jo was thankful no other cars had been on the road when the Mercury went into its spin. She rested her head on the steering wheel, not sure whether to laugh or cry.

"Thank God," her voice wavered. "We're alive, Gracie. Are you okay?"

She reached over to Grace's arm, and became frantic when she saw her sister slumped against the side window. "Sissie?" she yelled as she tugged on her sister. "Gracie?" but Gracie didn't respond. A large goose egg had begun to form on Grace's forehead. *Oh, Gracie, don't do this to me now.*

Jo took a huge breath, squeezed her eyes tight, and silently breathed a prayer. "God, I've never talked to you before, and maybe now isn't a good time to start, but we really need your help. My sister needs your help. Please, God."

Jo's arm muscles were tense and sore as she urged the car back into its proper lane. So close to the edge, one small misdirection would send them into the ditch on the other side. Snowdrifts acted as a barrier and helped give leverage. Finally, the Mercury turned around and they began to crawl north again. After some time, Grace regained consciousness.

"Oooh...." groaned Grace; she held her head in her hands. "My head hurts. What happened?"

"We were almost in a terrible wreck, Sissie. How do you feel?"

"Bad headache," she tried to laugh, but it came out as a sick groan. "Are we close to Dol's?"

"About fifteen miles, but it's hard to see through the snow. Are those taillights up ahead?"

Grace squinted through the iced-up windshield. "Looks like cars are stopped. Slow down."

"Looks like a parking lot for miles! Look! The snow has drifted around several cars. They're getting packed in."

"No one is moving," Grace shivered as they neared the other cars. She retrieved her coat from the backseat and pulled it tight around her. She grabbed Jo's arm, her eyes big with fear. "Jo, what are we going to do? We can't just sit here. We'll be stranded too."

"Maybe we should pray, Sissie." Jo's voice was calm and reassuring. "God can see us through this." Jo hoped she had spoken the truth.

Dol paced the floor, peered out the window, and worried about her sisters driving on the road in the middle of a Nebraska blizzard. Midwest winters could get wicked in a hurry. She called Ben again. He reported roads had drifted over where he worked in Fremont too. He said he might have to stay at the office until the roads were cleared. Dol fretted.

Four hours after Jo and Grace left Lincoln, they pulled into Dol's drive – shaken, but thankful to be alive and safe.

"What a horrendous trip!" Jo exclaimed as she met Dol at the door.

Dol greeted them with hugs, and hurried them inside out of the blowing snow. "I knew God would protect you, but honestly? I was worried too. I'm so glad you're both safe and sound." She examined Grace's forehead. "What happened to you?"

They told her about the roads, the narrow escape from a horrible accident, and almost sliding into the ditch. Dol examined the bruise, and then got an ice pack.

"Guess I now have 'something blue' for the wedding," Grace moaned. "Hope it goes away by then."

"It was really strange, Dol," Jo recalled. "We were in the middle of the gridlock a few miles south of Fremont; cars were stranded in front of us. We couldn't go anywhere, but also knew we couldn't afford to be stranded."

"That's when Jo prayed," Grace added.

Dol arched her eyebrows in question.

"And that's when it happened...."

CHAPTER 38 - SNOWBOUND

"It was a miracle, Dol! We sat in the car frightened as we watched the snow swirl around us, packing us in inch by inch. We realized we had no blankets to keep us warm, or food to eat if we became stranded. The only thing we could think to do was pray, and then God provided a miracle! That's the only way I can describe it."

Grace nodded, her eyes still large with astonishment. "It was really something!"

"Well, go get warmed up by the fireplace. I'll get some hot chocolate for you girls, and you can tell me all about it."

As they sipped their hot chocolate, Jo told the story. "A small car ahead of us slowly pulled out onto the oncoming lane. It appeared no cars were coming, but it was difficult to see in the near whiteout. Strangely, I felt a brave confidence to follow."

"I screamed at her," admitted Grace. "But she said, 'if he can do it, so can I,' and she pressed on the gas and followed the leader — on the *wrong side* of the road! We passed dozens of cars slowly being eaten up by the swirling white snow monster. Believe me, even I prayed!"

"For another long hour, we inched forward mile by mile, following the little car, until we reached an impasse where the road turns off I-77 in Fremont onto Route 30 toward your house. A line of southbound cars met the stranded caravan going north. The smallest margin of space existed between the cars on the opposing lanes. I stayed behind the small car as close as I dared, and marveled as it slipped through the opening. Our Coupe was slightly wider, but I prayed and dared to follow."

"Honest to God, I don't know how we squeezed through that tight opening! I almost had a hissy fit. What if we had gotten stuck? Jo told me to pray and have faith, so I closed my eyes tight and prayed until Jo said we were through." Grace shivered as she retold the story.

Dol wiped at unbidden tears as she heard the girls' amazing account. Silently, she thanked her Lord for protecting her sisters.

Jo continued. "After we got through the opening, I pulled the car back on the right side of Route 30 going east. It was only a few more miles to your place. The road was clear of cars; we had the snowy road to ourselves."

"What happened to the little car?" Dol asked.

"Dol, it disappeared!" Grace's eyes were wide. "Snow blew sideways, and so dense it was hard to see, but all of a sudden, it was just – gone. Gone! We didn't see it turn off anywhere!"

"Girls, sometimes God compels us to pray. Today was one of those days. I was worried sick about you until the Lord reminded me of a very important fact: you were both in His hands. He would take care of you. So I asked God to keep you safe, and for faith to believe He could. My part – the hardest part – was to trust that He would."

They nodded in agreement, still dumbfounded at the miracle they had just experienced.

Dol looked out the window. "By the looks of things outside, you may be here for a few days. Good thing I went shopping yesterday. I called Ben and found out he's snowed in at his office in Fremont. I've wanted to spend quality time with my sisters, and it looks like now we're going to have our special girl-time together. I'm excited about that!"

Little Molly heard her mother as she came into the room. "Girl-time? What about baby Timmie? Can he be a part of girl-time too?"

"I'm sure he won't mind, Sweetie," Jo laughed as she picked up the baby and tousled his hair. "We're going to have fun together."

Grace suddenly became anxious. "Dol, will you have time to finish all the dresses? The wedding's only a couple weeks away!"

"There were five to make: mine, Jo's, my two girls', and yours. That's not many for me, Grace." Dol's warm smile comforted Grace. "Plus, my best friend, Jenna, has helped me a lot. You remember her from the orphanage, don't you? All I really have left to do on the dresses is to have you try them on and see if they need any tucks, measure them for length, and then hem them."

"Mama, can we show Auntie Grace our dresses?" Lizzie asked.

"Grace, the girls are tickled to death that you want them for your flower girls. It's all they can talk about."

"I'd love to see them!" Grace bubbled and clapped her hands. "This wedding will be more wonderful than any I ever dreamt of before!"

Lizzie and Molly squealed with delight and ran to their bedroom to don their dresses. Dol went to help them.

"Almost everyone in the family will be a part of my wedding!"

"Dol and me as bridesmaids, the little girls as flower girls, big brother Guy to walk you down the aisle...." Jo went over the list. "And if Frank comes down from Wisconsin, we'll all be together again."

"Oh no! I haven't even asked him yet...." Grace was interrupted as Lizzie pranced out of the bedroom. The girl twirled circles before Grace, fascinated as her wine-colored chiffon dress swirled around her. Three-year-old Molly tried the same trick and stumbled on the long skirt.

Grace put her hand to her heart. "Oh! The girls are so precious, and the dresses are gorgeous. I love the extra-special touches you've put on them."

"Jo's and my dresses are similar to the flower girls', except the skirts won't be as full. And now, baby sister—" she paused with dramatic flair, "Are you ready to see your wedding gown?"

Grace's eyes grew large. "You've already begun to make it?"

Dol nodded.

"You should have seen some of the atrocities Mother made me try on. There was one I loved, but it was very expensive."

"You showed me at the bridal shop, remember?" She led Grace to the couch. "Sit here and wait. I'm going to help the girls out of their dresses before they tear or dirty them. I'll be right back."

Grace and Jo were still talking about contacting Frank when Dol returned with Grace's wedding gown on a silk-covered hanger.

"What do you think, Gracie?"

"Ooooh, Dolly...." She covered her mouth and squealed. "It's absolutely gorgeous! She jumped to her feet and fondled the ivory satin between her fingertips. The gown was simple but elegant with covered buttons down the back. "It's – it's just perfect! William will faint for sure," Grace giggled. "Can't wait to see his face!"

"Do you think Frank will agree to come down for the wedding? I haven't even asked him about it yet."

"It's a long drive from Wisconsin, but I'm sure he wouldn't miss it. Our whole family needs to together for this gala event," Dol agreed.

"There may be a way," Grace nodded as she scratched her head. "You said he'd become a minister, right?"

Jo laughed. "Grace always scratches her head when she gets an idea. It's like she has to catch it before it disappears from her brain."

Dol smiled at the thought and nodded.

"Can we call him?" Grace asked.

The girls huddled around Dol as she dialed Frank's number. Grace held the receiver away from her ear so Dol and Jo could listen in.

"Hi, Frank – or should I call you Father Frank?"

"Just Frank to you, baby sister," he laughed. "I hear you're getting married – beating all of us to the altar, are you?"

She giggled. "Frank. I was going to be married in a large cathedral in Lincoln with a priest I didn't even know, but those plans fizzled out. So now I need someone to perform the ceremony. Dol says you're a minister, so would you marry me?"

"I'm your brother, Grace, I can't marry you."

She giggled as she heard the tease in his voice. "Then, would you do the honors of performing my ceremony? Does that sound better?"

"You mean, I'm your backup plan?" he laughed. "When is it? Will it still be in Lincoln?"

"New Year's Eve, December 31st – and no. We've decided to hold a small family wedding at Dol's church here in Arlington. We want it to be a family affair. If you can come, our family will be complete."

"Grace, I would be more than honored to marry you and your man. In fact, it will be my first wedding, so I can practice on you." He chuckled again.

Grace wasn't sure if he were serious or not. "That's swell, Frank. I hope you bring Anne. Dol has told us all about her. I'm anxious to meet her."

"I'll see if I can twist her arm to come with me."

She hung up the receiver. "He said he'd do it!" Grace squealed. "We're all going to be together again."

The blizzard raged and became one of the worst Nebraska had seen in years. The sisters paid no attention as snowdrifts mounted around the house. They were warm and safe even though they were snowbound in the rural Arlington home. Dol kept them busy with baking for the holidays, sewing, fitting dresses, and chatter.

Dol told them how she and Ben had met and fell in love; they talked about their two younger brothers who had died and wouldn't be at the family reunion. They laughed and cried, and chattered like schoolgirls.

Wedding preparations were almost complete, Christmas was right around the corner with a promise to have everyone for dinner, and Grace was on cloud nine.

CHAPTER 39 - CHRISTMAS DAY

Christmas Day festivities brought joy that only a reunited family could bring. Weather threatened to hamper the day with another storm, but squalls soon diminished and the group was off. Guy drove the group north to Arlington for the promised Christmas dinner, and another family gathering.

Grace brought William to meet the family. Since Jack's family was in California, he came along too, to Jo's delight. She was happy for the opportunity to get to know him better.

"Guy, you're the lone duck out," Grace teased. "We'll have to see what we can do about that."

Dol greeted them at the door and welcomed them in. Lizzie and Molly were quick to grab their aunties' hands and pull them into the living room to show them the festive Christmas decorations. Warm aromas of pumpkin pie and fresh-baked bread permeated the house.

"Mmmm-mmmm. I'm drooling already! Don't remember the last time I had a *good* piece of pumpkin pie." Guy licked his lips, cocked his head with a goofy gesture at Dol, and grinned.

Dol gave him a playful punch on the arm, "A few weeks ago, silly. Have you forgotten

Thanksgiving dinner already?" she laughed. "Also have your favorites: apple and pecan."

"Just playin' with you, Dol," he smirked. "I know they're all delicious." He smacked his lips again and gave her a good squeeze.

She hugged him in return and shook hands with the other men as they were introduced. "Ben is in the other room. Go ahead and join him, and get acquainted. We'll call you men when it's time to eat. Girls, come help me in the kitchen," Dol beckoned.

They were surprised to see another young lady at the kitchen counter mashing potatoes.

"Remember Jenna?" asked Dol.

Jo's eyes brightened in recognition. "Yes, I remember you, Jenna. You were at the orphanage with us; whenever we saw Dol, we saw you."

"We became very good friends. In fact, more like sisters. Dol has been good to me, Josie. She's given me a home, a job, and a family. I could never repay her kindness."

"You're family, Jenna." Dol waved her off. "Jenna was the one who taught me how to sew when we were at the orphanage; that's what helped me get my apprenticeship with Mrs. Hendricks."

"But then it was you, Dol, who persuaded Mrs. Hendricks to take me in when I turned thirteen. You knew I had nowhere else to go."

"Jenna's parents were killed in a car accident, so we grew up together. Violet Hendricks, whom we called Ma Hendricks, took us both in. We lived there and worked for her sewing business. Now Jenna works for me at my *Seen It Sewn It Shop.*"

Jenna hugged Grace. "Grace. I'm so happy to help with your wedding dresses. It's been sheer pleasure. And Jo, how about you? What are your plans?"

The question caught Jo off-guard. "You mean about marriage?" She snickered, flustered. "Haven't thought about that yet. Have to find the right man first."

Grace gave her a playful shove. "Don't tell me you don't have your eyes on Jack, Jo. I've seen how ruffled you get around him."

Jo shot her a dirty look and changed the subject. "I don't know how much Dol has told you, Jenna, but I plan to enter Nebraska State in the spring for nursing classes. And I've applied at the hospital in Huskerville for a nurse's aide position. So keep your fingers crossed."

"I'll do better than that," replied Jenna. "I'll pray God works things out for you – for the job and for college."

"How's the house coming along, Will?" Ben asked. "I understand you're fixing up a little place for you and Grace outside Lincoln?"

"Yes sir. Coming right along, sir," William nodded.

"No need to call me sir," Ben laughed. "You'll soon be my brother-in-law, and part of the family."

William gave a stiff smile. "We probably could have afforded a fancier place, but Grace and I want to start out simple and build our way up."

"Smart man, this one," Guy nodded with approval. "Ben, whatever happened to that Smarkel lady at the orphanage?"

Ben chuckled. "She got herself into deep water with all the funds she had accepted from John McMillan. He extorted those funds, but she accepted them, which made her an accessory to the crime. She'll spend time in prison too. In fact, all of Overbrook's policies are being reviewed and the books are being audited. A lot more may have been going on in the orphanage than we care to know."

Guy shook his head. The men went on to fill in the story for William and Jack.

"And Jo's adoptive father had her official records all along, huh? What a wonderful guy," Jack's voice dripped with sarcasm.

"He's in prison for good long time," said Ben. "And all his financials are being audited as well. It doesn't look good for him."

"How does this information affect you, Will?" Guy noticed the man's face looked strained. "You're not going to get cold feet and back out on my sister now, are you?"

"It's all a surprise and a shock, that's all. I always thought Mr. McMillan was an outstanding citizen in the community. He had offered me a top job in his company. Of course, that's out now. It's hard to believe he would stoop to such conduct," William replied. "I'm more than anxious to get my Grace out of that place! I'm glad she moved in with Jo when she did."

"What will you do for work...?"

Molly interrupted. "Daddy, Mama says dinner is ready. Come on, let's eat," she tugged on his hand to pull him up.

They gathered around the abundant table spread with a huge turkey and all the trimmings. Mealtimes were much different since the war had ended. Food rations were not as strict; flour, dairy products, and produce were more plentiful, and Dol's table proved it. She had prepared a feast.

Guy's eye perked up at the bronze beauty with raven-black hair who brought the bowl of mashed potatoes to the table.

"Gentlemen, I want you to meet my best friend, Jenna. She is my 'sister' from the orphanage. Since she has no family except for ours, I invited her to join us. Jenna, this is my brother, Guy, his friend Jack, and Grace's husband-to-be — in only one week!" Her voice rose a pitch as she grinned at Grace, "Jenna, this is William.""

Jenna shook their hands and greeted each of them. Guy was taken by her. He held on to her hand a little longer than he should have. Jenna felt his gaze upon her and blushed. She meekly pulled her hand away and took her seat at the table.

Dol had cleverly seated them in couples: William with Grace, Jack by Jo, and Guy by Jenna. Guy caught his sister's eye and winked with a nod of approval.

"Perfect, Dol. This is perfect."

"Matchmaker," Ben mouthed at him. "Guy, would you do the honors and say grace?"

"More than honored, Ben. I am so thankful for this family."

"Before we open presents, we have a special tradition in the Ryan household," Ben announced. "Let's gather in the living room around the Christmas tree to read the Christmas story. Lizzie, would you get Daddy's Bible?"

The group assembled in the living room with their pie and coffee, and had just sat down when they heard a blood-wrenching scream from the other room.

Dol and Ben both ran to find Lizzie on the floor next to a toppled stool, holding her arm. The Bible lay on the floor next to a broken gift.

"I'm sorry, Mama," she whimpered.

"Lizzie! What in the world...?" Dol examined her daughter's arm and saw that it was rotated the wrong way. Lizzie screamed as her mother tried to touch it.

"Don't touch it, Mama! It hurts!"

Ben gently lifted his daughter from the floor and hurried out to the car. Dol grabbed their coats and followed close behind while the rest gawked, asking what happened.

"Lizzie fell. Broke her arm," Dol's words were clipped. "Closest doctor's in Fremont."

"Go," said Guy. "We'll wait until you come back."

"Don't worry about the kids, Dol. We'll take care of things here."

"Now what?" moaned Grace. "Lizzie's my main flower girl. How can she toss petals with a broken arm?"

C. A. Simonson

CHAPTER 40 - WEDDING DAY

Grace and Jo decided to spend the week between Christmas and New Year's at the Ryan home. They could help with final preparations for the wedding and help take care of the children. Lizzie was brought home wearing an arm cast to protect her forearm which had broken in two places.

"I'll never be a flower girl now," she moaned.

"We'll fix it, Lizzie," her mother assured her.

Frank and Anne arrived midweek, and the family reunion began anew as Frank reunited with his younger sisters. Stories were shared and the house was full of activity, fun, and warmth.

"Are you sure there will be enough food for everyone?" Grace was beside herself with worry. "Are the flowers on their way? Do you think I sent out enough...?" She scratched her head as she recounted numbers in her head.

"Grace, Grace," calmed Dol. "Everything is taken care of. Don't worry. It'll all turn out just fine."

"Oh, no!" Grace clapped her hands over her mouth with a 'I-just-remembered-what-I forgot' look. "What about the cake? I forgot all about the cancellation on the cake in Lincoln!"

Dol laughed. "Like I said, don't worry. Ma Hendricks has offered to bake the wedding cake as a wedding gift to you."

"The reception? The food?"

"Sissie, you know Dol has it all under control. She's the best."

Grace plopped down in the overstuffed chair. "I know. I'm a wreck. What if something else goes wrong?"

"What more do you want to happen, Sissie?" Jo threw her hands in the air. "I think we've all had our share of bad luck to last a lifetime."

"Will Joan McMillan be here for the wedding?" Dol asked with a hint of caution.

Jo frowned at the question, but Grace didn't notice.

"No, I don't think so. I would've liked for her to be here, but she's still recuperating in the hospital. Her nerves were shot after all she'd been through. To find out the man you've lived with for years wasn't at all who he said he was — well, that was a jolt to her. She was always on the jittery side anyway. The news of his conviction and arrest broke her. It may be a long time before she's well."

"I'm sorry to hear that, honey. Someday, you may have the opportunity to introduce her to the One who will bring her perfect peace, not only for her mind, but for her heart as well."

Grace thought a moment, and then nodded her understanding.

December 31st dawned bright and clear. William and his groomsmen had driven to Fremont the night before and stayed in Mrs. Hendricks' home. The Ryans' had a full house, but found room for Guy and Jack in their four-bedroom home with the girls doubling up.

The wedding was scheduled for three o'clock in the afternoon. Grace's nerves were on edge as Jo took the last of the bobby pins out of her pin curls.

"I don't know if I can go through with this," Grace's face wrinkled in worry and doubt.

"Grace! What are you talking about? Everything's ready and in place. It's just your nerves talking," Jo scolded.

"But what if...what if Will is...is like Father? What if he becomes the kind of man who treats me like Father treated Mother?"

"Don't even think such a thing, Sissie. It's bad luck on your wedding day."

Dol overheard their conversation while putting the finishing touches on Lizzie's and Molly's hair. She came over and began to massage Grace's shoulders. "Sweet Grace, you worry way too much. William is a good man, as far as I can tell. He's a hard worker, a good thinker, and most of all, he loves you with all his heart. He wants nothing more than to provide for you," said Dol. She felt Grace relax under her touch.

"You always know what to say, Dol," Grace hugged her sister's neck. "Thanks for being here for me."

"Always, honey," Dol squeezed back. "Now, let me style your hair and make you the perfect bride."

"I can't find the ring," William whispered to Guy as they arrived at the church. "Grace will never forgive me! What will I do?" He dug through his pockets for the fourth time. "I don't know what I did with it."

"Let's ask Frank. He'll know what to do." Guy had never seen a man with such bridegroom jitters before. "At least you brought yourself."

"Hey, Father Frank," Guy patted his younger brother on the back. "I love to call you that," he laughed. "Seems our new brother-in-law-to-be has a little problem." He put his arm around William's shoulder.

"Don't know how I could be so dumb," William confessed as he shook his head. "Must have forgotten the ring back home. I can't find it anywhere. I can't go back and get it now. What should I do?"

"First of all, calm down," Frank smiled. "It's no

problem. We'll figure it out."

"You're a lifesaver, Frank. I hope Grace will understand. Feel like such a dope. What a way to start a marriage."

"If that's the worst it gets, you'll be a fortunate man, Will."

The little church started to fill up with friends and family. Jack, Ben, and Anne took their seats. Jenna joined them and saved an outside space for Guy. The music began to play.

"About ready, Sissie?" Jo called to Grace as she checked her own image in the mirror. The gown fit perfectly. "Dol, this is one of the most beautiful dresses I have ever owned. You did a fantastic job!"

Lizzie and Molly could hardly contain their excitement in their new dresses. Their long hair curled in multiple ringlets after Dol had wrapped the girls' hair in rags the night before. She had tied their hair back with wine-colored ribbons and told them to sit still until it was time to walk down the aisle.

"The music is starting, Sissie."

Dol noticed Grace at a standstill in front of the mirror. She tiptoed up behind Grace and put her arm around her waist and felt the girl tremble. "Are you ready?" Dol whispered in her ear.

Grace squeezed her eyes tight and took a deep

breath. She nodded slightly and dared to look at Dol. A tear slipped down her cheek.

Dol hugged her tight. "Are you sure?" She cupped Grace's face in her hands and noted the anxiety in her face. "You'll be just fine, honey, trust me." Dol tucked a flowery band in Grace's hair as the final touch.

Grace took another big breath and nodded again. "I'm a bundle of nerves, but happy, that's all. I can't believe this is really happening."

Dol motioned for Jo and Grace to gather around her and grabbed their hands. "I want to pray for God's blessings on you Grace, before you become Mrs. Ericksen. God will take care of you and provide everything you need. Remember that. And no matter what, remember we'll always be your sisters."

Dol said a short prayer and as she said 'amen,' the wedding march began. Grace looked to her oldest sister for one more reassuring glance. Dol squeezed her hand and smiled with a nod.

"It's time girls," Dol beckoned to Lizzie and Molly. A chiffon wrap covered Lizzie's arm cast; she had arranged the wrap around the handle of a basketful of rose petals. "No one will ever know," she whispered in Lizzie's ear. "Molly, take your petals out of Lizzie's basket and stay by her side, okay?"

"I can go down by myself," Molly pouted. "I want my own basket."

Dol sighed inwardly. "Lizzie needs you today. You have to help her with the petals. Can you do that for Mama? For Auntie Grace?" She rubbed the little girl's back and nodded to encourage agreement.

Molly pouted, but nodded with reluctance. Dol sighed again. Getting Grace married had been one big chore, but she was so glad to have been there for her baby sister. She wouldn't have wanted anyone else to do it for her.

The music increased in volume, and everyone's heads turned to the back to watch as the bride came down the aisle. Grace looked up at Guy with a panicky smile. He grinned back and patted her arm interlaced with his. "Ready?" he mouthed.

Grace clung to Guy's arm half-afraid she would stumble, half-afraid she would faint. She felt his arm muscles through his shirt, and took courage at his strength. She knew he would be there for her too. As they stopped at the front, she looked into William's soft, loving eyes. This man had been there for her too. She yearned to be his wife – to be Mrs. Ericksen. She lifted her head and smiled as their eyes embraced one another.

Frank beamed with pride as he watched his brother and sister come up the aisle. His family was finally all back together in one place. He glanced at

the bridesmaids and flower girls. He looked out
into the audience and nodded at Ben. God was
good. Life was good. Now the bride and groom
were before him. It was time to begin.

"Who gives this woman to be married to this
man?" Frank asked.

"We do," Guy said. "Her brother and her
family."

A wondrous love radiated from Will as Grace
took his hand. She was now confident she was
marrying the man of her dreams. She squeezed his
hand as they made the final steps before the altar.

Frank provided a sermonette of encouragement
and advice for the couple. Remember," he concluded,
"Family ties are the most important bond you will
ever have. Do your best to keep them intact."

"Repeat after me. With this ring...."

William slipped the homemade paper ring onto
Grace's finger. "With this ring," he repeated and
looked at Grace with an 'I'm sorry' look.

"I thee wed...."

"I thee wed." Grace stared at the paper ring and
a funny smirk crossed her lips. She glanced at Will.
He lowered his head with a slight shrug of his
shoulders and mouthed, "Forgot the ring."

Frank motioned to Will and Grace to join him
in the middle of the platform. A platter holding a
goblet of wine along with a small loaf of bread was
on a small table behind the altar.

"The bride and groom will now share in a private communion," he announced to the onlookers. "This is a moment they can share together as a couple in unity. While we perform this part of the ceremony, we ask that you enjoy the special music."

"Please kneel, while I pray over you," Frank asked the couple, "I will serve you communion."

Will and Grace knelt and bowed their heads in solemn reverence as the soloist began to sing. They began to hear people snicker all over the church. When Will and Grace dared to peek at each other, she gave him a questioning look. Frank said his prayer over the couple, and then calmly served them communion. He told them to remain kneeling until the song was finished. The snickering turned to giggles and Grace felt humiliated. *What's so funny?* She questioned Frank with her eyes. He gave a slight shake of his head. She glared at Will, and he hung his head. "Sorry," he mouthed as they stood.

"May I present to you Mr. and Mrs. William Ericksen." Grace was relieved to see a welcoming and joyful crowd applaud them on their way out.

The reception was small, consisting of simple cake and ice cream. "I know it's not the huge and grand banquet Mother wanted," Grace apologized to William. "None of it was as big as she wanted it to be."

"Maybe not, but it was ours, Grace, and it's perfect. I have you, and that's all that matters," Will kissed her forehead. "My turn to apologize. I'm so sorry about the ring. I rushed off yesterday and completely forgot it. We'll pick it up before we go on the honeymoon."

"I thought it was kind of funny. I like my paper ring." She smirked. "But what was going on during our communion? I was so embarrassed for the lady who sang. Her song was beautiful. Why would people laugh at her?"

"I heard she thought the same thing and almost walked out," he chuckled. "I've got something to show you." He pulled off his right shoe. "Look."

"It says, 'help'," Grace read.

"Yep. And the other one says 'please'. I knew it was there, but couldn't do a thing about it. The guys played a good joke on me."

"Did Frank know?"

"Don't think so – but Guy did, that rascal."

"Come on, Grace," called Jo. "Time to throw the bouquet. Make sure I get it, okay?"

Grace laughed. She'd noticed her sister holding hands with Jack. There was no one else she'd rather see get the bouquet—unless it was Jenna. She and Guy had exchanged flirting glances all day. Then there was Anne. Frank had been waiting a long time for his bride. How she loved this family. They were going to stick together forever through thick and thin.

The ladies were lined up anxious and excited, waiting to catch the bouquet.

Who'll be next? Grace turned around, closed her eyes, and tossed the roses over her head.

EPILOGUE

Thank you for reading the Journey Home Series. You may have wondered about the backgrounds of Frank and Dol. Mention was made of two younger brothers, Jo's twin brother, Jesse, and Mikie, who was two years younger than Frank.

Frank finds one brother, and then the other in the first book, only to lose them again to untimely deaths. The stories of their lives, and Mikie's horrible accident are told in *Love's Journey Home.* The first book also tells of Frank's coming of age, and his journey to find love and acceptance. You'll find why and how he ended up in Wisconsin and met Anne, the love of his life.

In Book II, *Love Looks Back,* Frank travels back home ten years later to search for his siblings as he struggles to reconcile Mikie's death with his conscience. Visiting the old homestead, he discovers his father's grave and what looks like a bloody murder in the barn. Following leads, he discovers a lot more than he had bargained for.

It also focuses upon Dol's journey, why she was forced to leave the orphanage, and how she met Ben. She and Frank find each other in a unique and touching way. Dol reveals how she struggled as her younger sisters were taken by the rich couple in the black sedan.

Together, Dol and Frank must pool their minds to figure out how and why their father was killed. The reader is left with clues as to why Guy left for war and the guilt he was trying to overcome.

Love's Journey Home and *Love Looks Back* are both available on Barnes and Nobel, Amazon and Smashwords in either paperback or in a variety of digital formats. You may also get a signed copy from https://casimonson.wordpress.com.

APPENDIX

This section is for the history buffs. The war stories in this book are based on true events which happened on the U.S.S. *Yorktown* in the Battle of Midway, 1942. The last battle became known as the "Miracle at Midway," and was possibly the most important battle of World War II according to Sir Winston Churchill.

The U.S.S. *Yorktown* was in a fierce battle on June 6, 1942, suffering five bomb hits which eventually sank the ship. The ship's remains still lie on the ocean floor of the South Pacific close to Hawaii. There were two men left on board, although history does not record their names nor their ranks. They were rescued the next day by the crew of U.S.S. *Hughes* when they shot rounds from a machine gun. Only one of the two men survived.

The U.S.S. Yorktown

Source: http://www.navsource.org/archives/02/021005.jpg; Public Domain
Photo of a Seaman of WWII, courtesy of C.A. Simonson

THE YORKTOWN – 1942

U.S.S. Yorktown on the morning of June 4, 1942 - USN - Official U.S. Navy photograph 80-G-21627-public domain-wikipedia.com

Fire on Deck-U.S.S. Yorktown-1942 -- Photographer 2nd Class William G. Roy - http://www.navsource.org/archives/02/05.htm - public domain

Yorktown is hit on the port side, amidships, by a Japanese Type 91 **aerial torpedo** during the mid-afternoon attack by planes from the carrier *Hiryu*.
https://en.wikipedia.org/wiki/USS_Yorktown

USN, photographed from USS *Pensacola* (CA-24) - Official U.S. Navy Photograph **80-G-414423**, U.S. National Archives.-Public Domain

---

Sources:

http://www.midway42.org/TheBattle/YorktownDamage.aspx
http://www.state-journal.com/local%20news/2011/06/07/yorktown-survivors-reunite
http://ww2db.com/ship_spec.php?ship_id=13
http://www.midway42.org/about_BOM.aspx
http://www.navy.mil/navydata/nav_legacy.asp?id=7
http://www.midway42.org/TheBattle/YorktownDamage.aspx
http://www.loc.gov/library/libarch-digital.html

HUSKERVILLE, NEBRASKA

On February 27, 1942, the U.S. Army chose Lincoln, Nebraska, to be the home of a new Air Force training base. The Engine Mechanics Technical School and Basic Training Center was located at Lincoln Army Air Field, Nebraska. The school focused on pilot training, technical training, basic training, and aircraft maintenance.

In the 1940s the 160-acre field sat on the northwest edge of some of Lincoln's salt flats near Oak Creek. Tens of thousands of fighter mechanics trained at Lincoln Army Air Field before World War II was over. The base was also the site of intensive heavy-bomber training.

The place became known as Huskerville. It grew so big so fast, it became its own city within a city. Huskerville supported thousands of returning GIs who attended the University of Nebraska on the GI Bill. The former base hospital for Lincoln Army Air Field located there was the State's largest hospital in terms of patients. Many students who attended the University of Nebraska lived in the small apartments on base. It was complete with barracks, training centers, an airbase, stores, a hospital, a grocer, theater and many apartments.

---

http://www.lincolnafb.org/history.php
http://wikimapia.org/10023460/Huskerville

THE BURR BLOCK

Where McMillan's Industries Corporate offices were located

The Burr Block, also known as the Veterans Administration Building, is historically significant to Lincoln architecture. Originally constructed in 1887, it was transformed twenty-nine years later into the modern ten-story skyscraper. It was known as the "Burr Block" of business activities in downtown Lincoln's main thoroughfare on O Street. The building has been known to house many significant businesses on the local, state and national levels.

http://www.lincolnafb.org/history.php

ABOUT THE AUTHOR

C.A. Simonson pens fiction and nonfiction. She has several award-winning short stories in anthologies, and many nonfiction articles in newspapers, magazines, and blogs. By writing, she hopes to encourage and inspire, and perhaps get the reader to delve into their own soul for true answers.

She is the mother of two grown sons and grandmother to six grandchildren. When she is not writing, she loves to craft, play piano, paint, or fish in their backyard pond. She lives in southern Missouri.

Friend her on Facebook:
https://www.facebook.com/CASimonson
Follow on Twitter:
https://twitter.com/candysimonson
Connect on LinkedIn:
http://www.linkedin.com/pub/candace-simonson

Read more stories and get news about books at:
http://casimonson.wordpress.com
http://candysimonson.wordpress.com
http://kitchentipsandtreasures.wordpress.com

C. A. Simonson

Made in the USA
Charleston, SC
30 November 2015